President Vladimir Putin and us

Åse Thomassen

President Vladimir Putin and us

Åse Thomassen

ISBN: 9798327795679

Protence Publishing

Oslo, Norway

Content

CONTENT   3

PRESIDENT PUTIN AND US   7

    INTRODUCTION   7
    WHAT DOES PUTIN COMMUNICATE IN HIS SPEECHES?   9
    TALIBAN, BUT NOT RUSSIA OR PUTIN   11
    A BREAKDOWN IN COMMUNICATION   12
    BETWEEN WARHAWKS AND THE TRUTH   14

INTRODUCTION   19

PRESIDENT VLADIMIR PUTIN – FROM A BOY TO PRESIDENT OF RUSSIA   23

    INTRODUCTION   23
    BACKGROUND   24
    THE THUG FROM LENINGRAD   25
    EDUCATION AND CAREER   26
    PUTIN TODAY   28
    A MACHIAVELLIAN LEADER?   30
    PRESIDENT, DICTATOR, OR AUTOCRAT?   31
    PUTIN AND DEMOCRACY   32
    AN ENIGMA   33
    SUMMARY   34

PROPAGANDA   37

    INTRODUCTION   37
    FACTS AND FICTIONS   39

The context of propaganda   40
When the propaganda meet reality   42
The triplets of propaganda   43
Propaganda through narratives   44
A clash in communication?   45
Summary   45

PUTIN`S SPEECH IN MUNICH IN 2007   **47**

Introduction   47
What does the speech actually say?   47
The speech at the Munich Conference on Security policy   49
What does the speech convey?   72
The beginning of the speech   73
The message in the speech   74
The speech as rhetoric   75
Absence of rhetorical devices   76
Summary   77

SPEECH FEBRUARY 24,2022   **79**

Introduction   79
The speech   79
The perspective and the message   98
The rhetoric of the speech   99
A strong and ambiguous threat   101
Summary   103

THE INTERVIEW WITH TUCKER CARLSON?   **105**

Introduction   105
The interview   106
What can we learn from the interview?   110
Summary   111

SPEECH AFTER THE TERROR ATTACK IN THE CROCUS CITY HALL   **113**

INTRODUCTION 113
THE SPEECH 113
WHAT DOES PUTIN EMPHASIZE IN HIS SPEECH? 118
SUMMARY 119

PUTIN ON ESCALATION **120**

INTRODUCTION 120
PUTIN WORDS ABOUT ESCALATION 120
A CLEAR MESSAGE. CALM AND ANGRY 122
QUESTIONS FROM PRESIDENT PUTIN TO THE WEST 123
IMPORTANT QUESTIONS ABOUT A POSSIBLE FURTHER ESCALATION 124
SUMMARY 124

US AND PRESIDENT PUTIN **126**

INTRODUCTION 126
HEGEMONIC THINKING IN THE WEST 126
PRESIDENT YELTSIN 128
THE WAR IN IRAQ – THE BEGINNING OF A NEW HOSTILITY BETWEEN
RUSSIA AND THE US 129
THE WAR HAWKS (NEOCONS) 129
EUROPE IN DENIAL? 131
SUMMARY 133

SUMMARY **135**

A PRISON OF ARGUMENTS 137
TRUTH AND PROPAGANDA 137

REFERENCES **140**

CONCEPTS IN RHETORIC **151**

President Putin and us

Introduction

Why do we not understand the speeches of President Putin? Why do we not catch his message in the Western part of the world? How do the misunderstandings arise in the communication between President Putin and the West? Have – the collective West- even tried?

With us I mean US, NATO, EU, Europe, and alliances of the West. There are many indications that the war in Ukraine is perceived differently in countries outside the West.

There is an uncomfortable climate in which to study the war in Ukraine, President Zelensky and President Putin. Since the invasion of Ukraine, the term traitor has not only been about betraying one`s country. It has been enough to question the narratives about the war in Ukraine.

In Norway, tolerance for dissenting opinions about Vladimir Putin has been low since the invasion of Ukraine on February 24, 2022. As a matter of fact, we find the lack of tolerance for dissenting opinions regarding Ukraine in most Western countries.

In a situation where there is and was a risk for the outbreak of the third world war, it is important to understand what President Vladimir Putin expresses and means. We cannot afford not to. It is tragic that the West is more concerned with demonizing president Putin than finding solutions that might bring peace. I say this without being naïve. I know the background of the proxy war taking place in Ukraine. The Western narrative of the war in Ukraine is different from the facts about the war and the background for the war.

President Putin is controversial in the West, to say it mildly. For many, the invasion of Ukraine became the very proof that he is evil. Few are interested in what Putin actually says. What he means. It is as if what he says to the West passes through a filter of negativity. If it weren`t for the fact that the situation was so serious, it would be absurd. How can we close our ears to one of the world's most important leaders? How can we in the so-called West not listen to President Putin? Or read him like the devil reads the bible.

We don`t really have the luxury of refusing to listen to Putin. Still his words seem almost as a greater taboo than the worst pornography. How did we end here? Perhaps this is most of all a terrible mixture of propaganda, groupthink, and human laziness. The propaganda has an extra strong effect when many people do not want to examine the facts of the case and think accordingly.

What does Putin communicate in his speeches?

My ambition is to say something about President Putin and what he conveys in some selected speeches. There are many who will object that we should not believe Putin`s words. Then I would say: Do we have an alternative to interpreting his speeches and his words?

A Norwegian journalist said that if you take a lie detector test on Putin, the electricity will go off in all of Moscow. One can interpret this as truth or an exaggeration - a rhetorical hyperbole. In any case, the journalist gives a very dark picture of the possibility of interpreting Putin based on what he says. I will do it- even though many will think that it is impossible or unnecessary. We really don`t have an alternative to listening to President Vladimir Putin`s words. He is one of the worlds` most important heads of state. Many politicians in the West talk about him as if he is a mad dog who leads a banana republic. It`s not just crazy or stupid, but also downright destructive.

I find many of Putin`s speeches both thorough and logical. In this book, Putin`s words have the same value as banknotes. This means that what Putin says is what he means.10 dollars is ten dollars. Many will object to such an approach. Many would call it naive. However, I believe that the West has made a catastrophic mistake by ceasing to listen to President Putin, and neither be in a dialogue with him. It seems that the West has blocked itself from knowledge, wisdom, and dialogue about the war. President Putin is the key to a better relationship between the West and

Russia. Ignoring him is the least constructive thing the West has done for a long time.

Taliban, but not Russia or Putin

Norway has taken pride in treating the Norwegian terrorist Anders Behring Breivik humanely. He killed 77 people, most of them children and young people, in 2011. That he destroyed the government quarter was nearly a trifle compared to the murder of many children and young people. The most destructive Norwegian since the second World War has three rooms in prison. He has even been allowed to criticize the authorities for their treatment of him in court several times. As far as Behring Breivik is concerned, the willingness to find humane solutions has been great. When it comes to President Putin, both Norwegians and the rest of the West seem uninterested in the slightest hint of understanding what he says. The former Norwegian foreign minister, Anniken Huitfeldt, invited Taliban to Norway few months after they were back in power in Afghanistan. She wanted to talk with Taliban, but not with Russia, which is partly crazy since Norway depend on a good relation to our neighbor Russia.

If enough people try to understand what Putin is saying, then we probably can conduct debates and policies in line with what`s a sensible policy for the US, NATO, and countries in Europe. Today, the understanding of Putin and his words is disturbed by the many characteristics about him. The negative propaganda about President Putin is like a window that has not been cleaned for several years. Then it is often difficult or impossible to see through the window.

A breakdown in communication

This book is based on this model of communication:

The Observers	Noise in communication	President Putin
Heads of state Researchers Editors The global public	Propaganda Knowledge Prejudices Values Groupthink (The West is the good guy)	The strategy of Russia The strategy of the President of Russia, Putin Personal characteristics What he says What he does

Fig.1 A model of communication

It has been a breakdown in communication, especially in the first two years of the war in Ukraine. I am not saying that Putin is white as snow. My message, however, is that we must see Putin as he presents himself. This is not about naivety. On the other hand, it is about a willingness to understand the message of Russia`s powerful leader. What does he mean?

Most people observe President Putin through the media. Most people have a limited impression of Putin. He is not a politician who invites the spectators to his home or participates in soft talk shows where you are expected to talk about your life, your cat, or a terrible event in life.

The war in Ukraine is terrible. No doubt about it. Russia attacked its neighbor. The US and NATO might have prevented it, but they chose zero communication before the war. Silence is also a choice. There was no response to President Putin`s proposal in December 2021. Two months before the Russian invasion. US and NATO had a choice. They could in fact have prevented the war. It shouldn`t have been a difficult choice. Whatever what one may think of what could lead to a war. The United States bears a great responsibility in opting out of communication with Russia in the months leading up to the war.

Russia is not a democracy in the Western sense. Russia does not have a form of governance equivalent to the leading Western democracies. At the same time, the United States has done much to undermine the authority of President Putin for more than twenty years. Many confuse what is about Russia, Russian democracy, or the absence of a Western democracy in Russia, President Putin and what that is relevant to understanding the war in Ukraine. The fact that leaders in the West want to weaken both President Putin and Russia as a state does not make it any easier.

Between Warhawks and the truth

The many issues about why there is a war in Ukraine make it difficult for both politicians and the population in the West to navigate between what is true and false, relevant, or irrelevant. War hawks like US senator Lindsay Graham do not hide their cynicism about the war in Ukraine. Other politicians speak with two voices. The first voice could be about creating support for the war in Ukraine as a defensive war for an independent country. The other voice may be about arguments

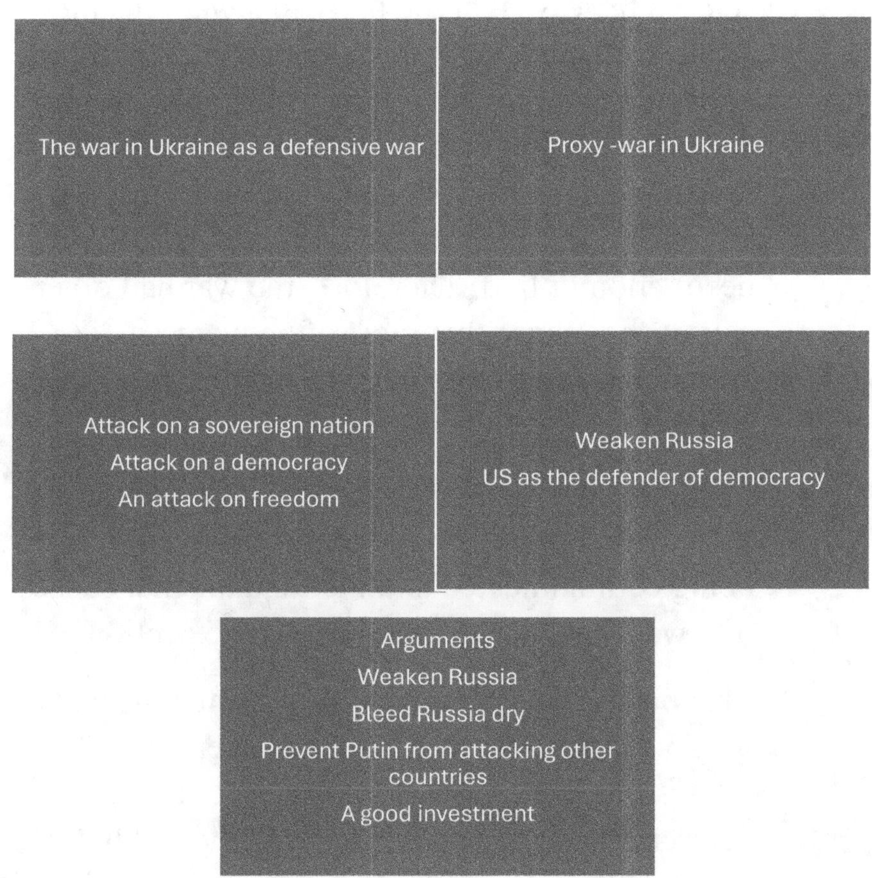

Fig.2 A model of the complexity of the war in Ukraine from a Western perspective

for a proxy war in Ukraine. For the Western public, it is difficult to understand what is what?

There are often complex reasons for wars. It`s seldom the case that the party to a war tells the whole truth about a war. There were for example many different justifications for the wars in Iraq and Afghanistan. Today, we know that the Americans' justification for the war in Iraq was based on a lie. There were no weapons of mass destruction in Iraq. Therefore, the war had other causes than those that most often were communicated to the public. That became common knowledge too late.

At the beginning of wars, it can be difficult for the population to distinguish between what is being communicated and the fundamental causes of a war. The war in Ukraine is no exception.

I have observed President Putin from a distance for 25 years. President Putin has been an interesting and unusual head of state for nearly a quarter of a century. The demonization of him in the West has grown progressively stronger since the US-led invasion of Iraq in 2003.

In Norway, governments have an attitude that we should talk to everyone. That includes the Taliban, Hamas, and the Houthi militia in Yemen. A willingness to talk to the most impossible is also a feature of the Norwegian society. In 2022, Norway followed America`s example and ruled out talking to Russia and Putin. In my opinion, this have been a thoughtless attitude in Norway, especially since we have had a good neighborly relationship with Russia, albeit with a high level of tension between 1945 and 1990. During the Cold war, the former Soviet Union was considered an enemy, although their efforts were crucial to an Allied victory over the Germans in 1945.

The Cold War between the former Soviet Union and the West must also be seen in the context of the former Soviet Union`s desire for expansion, and how they treated countries in Eastern Europe after the Second World War. There was a real fear that the former Soviet Union had ambitions beyond the countries of Eastern Europe. The Iron Curtain meant both a real and an ideological divide between the former Soviet Union and the West. After the fall of the Wall in Berlin in 1989, there was a unique opportunity for peace and reconciliation between the former countries of the Soviet Union and the West.

Here we are in 2024. We have been – and are- dangerously close to what could ignite a third world war. Nevertheless, we insist that Russia and Putin are black as the night, and that the West stands for the good values. Here, the West has locked itself into a world view that is not true. This book`s most important contribution – I hope- is to nuance the image of President Putin in the Western World.

The negative image of President Putin in the West undermines the fact that Putin has led the world`s largest country for 25 years and raised his two daughters together with his former wife. The daughters are successful in two different fields. A man without positive qualities would never been able to run a country and have a good family life. The West cannot afford only to see the black, caricatured side of Russia and President Putin. There are far more nuances regarding both President Putin and Russia. This book`s aim is therefore to provide a more balanced perspective of President Putin.

Introduction

I broke a convention by having the most important first chapter before this introduction to the book. I did that to invite the reader to accept the issue from the first page. Could it be that the way we look at President Putin have an impact on how we interpret him?

President Putin has often been portrayed as a "Hitler of our time" since 2014. Many still sees him exclusively as a Hitler and just evil-a person with a dream to be Peter the Great. But who is he - really?

In the West, we know little about the politician and the man Vladimir Putin. What does he emphasize? Who is he behind the screen of propaganda?

The next chapter is about Putin, only briefly. Our knowledge of President Putin is characterized by books and doctoral dissertations written by people who never have met President Vladimir

Putin. There are more claims, rumors, and theories than knowledge of who President Putin is. Many books are written about him, often with no ambition to analyze or understand who he is. There is a market for books about Putin that tell no news. Books that only consolidate the image of a horrible and cruel head of state. Most of the books lack exclusive knowledge of Putin. Few know much about him beyond biographical details. Anyway, authors and experts give the impression that they know him. Like me, they only have sources outside President Putin`s circle. My ambition in this chapter is to give a brief outline of who President Putin is. My knowledge of him is by no means exclusive. On the other hand, I want to give a truthful picture, as truthful as possible. I don`t want to make a cruel fantasy character just to sell books. My mission is to describe Putin in a way that creates interest. Knowledge of Putin has for far too long often been characterized by one-dimensional descriptions of Putin. The only thing I can say with 100 percent certainty is that Putin is not a one-dimensional person. Beyond that, I depend on other sources and my own observations of the leader of Russia, President Putin.

The understanding of propaganda is important for how we understand and misunderstand phenomena in international politics. The image that has been created about Putin is largely about propaganda. The second chapter is therefore about propaganda, and what characterizes propaganda.

Relations between Russia and the United States became increasingly worse after the Americans' insistence on invading Iraq. Russia, Germany, and France were against this war. The United States did not consider the objections of the other great powers. It has been argued that this disappointed President Putin. After the American invasion of Iraq, relations between the United States and Russia gradually worsened. What nevertheless formed a significant difference was Putin`s speech in Munich in 2007. The speech is commented in the fifth chapter.

In the sixth chapter, the speech from the first day of the invasion February 24, 2022, are analyzed as rhetoric. The core of the chapter is to look at President Putin`s words and rhetoric.

It has been written about Putin. He has been demonized. The first important interview in recent times was conducted by Tucker Carlson in February 2023. How can we understand this interview? What did President Putin actually say during this interview? And what was extraordinary about the interview? The interview was actually conducted in the heart of power in Russia, in the Kremlin.

There have been many claims that Putin wants to conquer Europe and the rest of the world. What can the speeches say about this? Is the picture of President Putin as Peter the Great just propaganda? Or do we soon need to change our glasses when analyzing and interpreting Putin?

Today, Putin is strongly demonized in the West. How can one distinguish between Putin`s words and actions and the propaganda about him?

Finally, there is an overview of terms in rhetoric and propaganda. These are particularly relevant for students and researchers who want to analyze Putin`s speeches and the propaganda about him.

President Vladimir Putin – from a boy to President of Russia

Introduction

The democracy in Russia is not perfect. Nor is the freedom of speech according to Western ideals. The fact that Russia does not score on the top level in terms of democracy and freedom of expression does not make Russia less valuable than countries that score higher in terms of degree of democracy and freedom of expression. Although I am a supporter of Western democracies, I see that we often look at other forms of governance with a kind of cultural arrogance. This contributes to us allowing ourselves to see Russia and President Putin as inferior to us. We can no longer afford this arrogance. President Putin has managed to lead the world`s largest country- Russia- for almost 25 years. When he took over, Russia was in a bad state economically.

In Western countries, Putin seems guilty of everything that is wrong with Russia. Even what is positive in Russia is described in negative terms. In this chapter I will give a brief overview of Vladimir Putin, the President of Russia. I want to interpret him with objective glasses. There are no more stupid than those who only want to convey President Putin as a master of evil. We need to ask better questions, and who is President Putin?

Background

While many political leaders in France and England have attended the same universities, Putin`s way to power is far more original. President Putin`s path to power is as remarkable as the fact that he has already led the world`s largest country for a quarter of a century. The fact that President Putin has led Russia for a quarter of a century is not just about power. The West`s one-dimensional image of Putin overshadows the fact that he has been able to lead the world`s largest country for 25 years. It requires other qualities than the negative ones that are emphasized in the West.

President Putin was born October 7,1952 in Leningrad (St. Petersburg). Putin was born seven years after the end of the Second World War. His family and Leningrad had suffered during the war. His parents had previously lost two children. Vladimir was therefore a beloved addition to the family, which was devastated by the impact of the Siege of Leningrad, the Second World War, the loss of his older brothers. Putin`s father suffered major injuries during the war. This meant that he was disabled and in great pain for the rest of his life. The city was still characterized by hunger, poverty, and aggression. Although he was born 7 years after the end of the war, the Second World War still cast a shadow over Sankt Petersburg and his family. It was only 8 years since the siege of Sankt Petersburg – then Leningrad- had ended. The hunger and the suffering during the Siege is unimaginable.

The thug from Leningrad

Putin is supposed to have nothing against the fact that it is known that he was a bully who fought a lot when he was growing up. It was a tough culture in the backyards of Leningrad. Even though he was small and stocky, he threw himself into one fight after another. At school he was considered a hopeless case. On the streets, however, all the fights gave Putin status.

When Putin was 13 years old, he began to take school more seriously. He joined the Young Pioneers, which was important for all pupils who wanted a good career in the Soviet society. In the 1960s, the Communist Party was the only political party in the former Soviet Union. Party affiliation meant a lot to the career. Background from the Young Pioneers in the Communist Party was therefore important.

Although Putin adapted to school and society from the age of 13, he continued to fight. He also made an effort with his schoolwork, so that he got good enough grades to be admitted to university.

Education and career

Putin studied Law at the Leningrad State University. He became a lawyer. He has never practiced law. Putin`s dream was never to become a lawyer. His dream was to become a spy in the KGB He was admitted to the spy school in Moscow where he received a different form of training than at the university.

Putin served 15 years for the KGB. He served six years in Dresden in former DDR, East Germany. He served in Dresden when the Wall went down in Berlin. He was lieutenant colonel when he retired from KGB in 1990.

Back in his hometown, he became prorector at the Leningrad State University. Shortly after that be became the adviser for the first democratically elected mayor of St. Petersburg. Putin then worked in the presidential staff in Moscow from 1996. Putin won great recognition in the staff of the President. The last day of December 1999, President Yeltsin announced his resignation. He appointed Putin as his successor.

Putin took over the leadership of a country that was on the brink of economic collapse. The transition to capitalism had resulted in a catastrophically poor economy in Russia. They had been exploited by Russian oligarchs and Western advisers. The latter thought more about their own profit than what was best for Russia.

President Yeltsin was popular in the West but he allowed Russia`s economy to be destroyed. Many Russians think of the 1990s as a terrible decade. Many did not get paid – even for months- while a few became very rich, nearly overnight.

Putin won his first presidential election in March 2000. Apart from the four years when Dmitrij Medvedev was president and Putin was prime minister in 2008-2012, Putin has led Russia since 2000. It is almost a quarter of a century. Early in his time as head of state, Putin carried out several reforms to improve Russia`s governance. He also demanded that the powerful oligarchs should stay away from politics.

Putin today

Although he turned 70 the year Russia invaded Ukraine in 2022, he does not appear to be an old man. He seems to be in good physical shape. For a man in his seventies, he appears to be at the height of his career. He is energetic, has a fast pace and can still give long speeches. At the same time, he is at an age where anything can happen. There is no obvious heir to the "throne".

If President Putin should be sick or die before his presidency is over in 2030, there is no clear successor to the current president. Although Russia is at war with Ukraine, Putin seems to be successful as the President of Russia. He also enjoys great respect in countries outside the West.

The Russian society is of course not perfect. Still, it is not as bad as it is made out to be in Western media. Much wealth is still concentrated in a few hands and the average standard of living is not as in prosperous Western countries. Still, it is much better than the worst propaganda about Russia. The internationally renowned Norwegian political scientist Stein Rokkan said that: "Votes count, resources decide". Translated into Russian conditions, one can say that the distribution of many of Russia`s resources took place in the 1990s. Even though President Putin has limited the political power of the oligarchs, they still have an unfair amount of Russia`s resources, Resources that should have been more wisely distributed in the decade before Putin became president.

A Machiavellian leader?

Niccolò Machiavelli has almost become a synonym for power, the understanding of power, promotion of power and abuse of power. While Machiavelli`s political philosophy was based on his experiences and observations from the city-state of Florence (The Prince), a similar book on Putin and his political leadership would be at least as interesting. The leader in the Kremlin must understand power like few others. This is not to say that Putin`s use of power is an example to follow. In any case, it is interesting how he has been able to retain power in 25 years, and most likely for years to come- if his health does not change the plans for Putin and Russia.

Today, a lot is known about management and leadership, but considerably less about political leadership and management. Often, analyzes of political leaders are superficial. In the media, emphasis is often placed on a political leader`s ability to communicate and his or her popularity. In the day-to-day work of the political leader, there are probably completely different abilities and skills that are more important in political leadership.

Researchers do not have access to Putin`s calendar, political relationships and people who are important for the understanding of Putin`s exercise of power. Individual stories and speculations are often understood as the truth. Although Putin undoubtedly wields power in a more brutal way than in the West, he is also undeniable a skilled chess player as Russia`s leader. Brutality and violence are probably far too easy and superficial explanations for Putin`s power in Russia, but it is these explanations that get attention in the West and characterize much of the thinking about Putin.

President, dictator, or autocrat?

It is often said that Putin is a dictator and autocrat. He has ensured that the electoral law was changed so that he can be president as long as the Russian people elect him. This would probably not have been possible if Putin was not such a popular leader in Russia.

Few if any in the West have sufficient insight into what is happening in Russian politics. Few can distinguish between legitimate exercise of power and illegitimate exercise of power in

Russian politics. On the other hand, it does no good underestimate Vladimir Putin because of the totalitarian features of the Russian society and its leadership.

Putin and democracy

President Putin is an extraordinary human being. An extraordinary politician. Not perfect. As head of state, he has brutal sides, often against opponents. The latter deserves a critical spotlight. In what way is President Putin hindering democracy and freedom of expression? However, this is just one of several parts of President Putin`s leadership. Although democracy is important, we cannot judge all other qualities to zero even if President Putin failed regarding a vibrant democracy in Russia. There are also many indications that the West is more concerned with democracy in Russia than the Russians themselves. It is also no secret that the US, through the CIA, has used resources on other politicians than Putin. That has hardly contributed positively to the development of democracy in Russia.

An enigma

Putin is probably an enigma. We know little about him. Before he became a politician, he worked for the secret services, KGB. Then it was important not to be noticed. We know little about Putin beyond biographical data.

Putin is a very private person. We don`t know if he was afraid of frogs when he was a child or if he had a heartbreak as a teenager. Russians who love their leader do it for who is – for them. The large minority who are not satisfied with Putin have limited information to criticize him for the human being he is. They can most of all criticize him for his policies and his strong power. However, the latter is difficult since there is not a vibrant political opposition in Russia. Although there is a formal system of governance in Russia, there is no doubt who is the most important person in Russia. However, those who make Putin and Russia the same are wrong. That the West imagines that Russia is led by a leader in a vacuum is a frequent fallacy in the West. President Putin's power rests on formal institutions such as the Russian Duma. Putin also surrounds himself with competent people.

Foreign Minister Sergej Lavrov is considered very capable.

For politicians in the West, Putin is probably most of all an enigma. There is no more than one version of Vladimir Putin. Putin is given many labels, diagnoses and he is compared with Adolf Hitler, Peter the Great and Russian tsars. Of course, Putin is a powerful leader of the world's largest country. He rules with a heavy hand- metaphorically speaking, but to call him Hitler, fascist or autocrat is superficial. For people in the West, Putin is probably most of all an enigma. Even highly intelligent people struggle to interpret Putin. It is difficult to find a category for Putin. Even if you like President Putin or not, he is a unique person. A unique politician. And for Western politicians most of all an enigma they struggle to understand.

Summary

This chapter on President Putin contains no news or sensationalism. However. I hope that I have made the reader consider Putin with more objective glasses. Putin is no saint, but he`s neither evil incarnate.

While little Peter is told that he must become friends with little Robert in kindergarten after a fight, there does not seem to be a corresponding demand for our leading politicians and media in the West. Therefore, the image of Putin as evil itself has been allowed to live without too many questions. President Barack Obama or President George W. Bush were never demonized like Vladimir Putin. Both started wars, but it did not have the same consequences as for Putin in the West.

President Putin is a rational leader of Russia. He emphasizes governance of Russia more than the introduction of a more Western democracy. The West has probably underestimated the leadership qualities of President Putin rather than having any interest in the leader of the world`s largest country.

There are few heads of state who have the same mental and intellectual capacity as Putin. It would be wrong to measure Putin solely on the degree of Western democracy in Russia. That it would have been desirable to have more democracy in Russia is of course desirable from a Western point of view – also from mine.

Judging President Putin based on a few variables is too easy. Leading Russia requires a complex set of leadership skills.

Propaganda

Introduction

Today, the term propaganda is used as if the term is explained and understood by everyone. That is partially misleading. How we understand the content of propaganda varies. It is about knowledge, cultural history, and prejudices. As well as the tendency to believe what we are told. Our understanding of President Putin is also about propaganda. To what extent is the individual able to distinguish between what he or she sees and hears from the propaganda about the same topic, event, or person?

Propaganda has a history of several hundred years, and probably further back in time. Where there has been a struggle for power, there has also been a struggle for the truth. Within our culture, the origin of the term propaganda is dated to 1622. Pope Gregory set up a committee of clergy that year. Their task was to spread the message of God based on the power of the word. Back then, propaganda was about spreading the word of God.

Techniques in propaganda

Appeal to threats
Appeal to fear
Appeal to dreams
Appeal to prejudices
Appeal to scapegoats (Jews, Muslims, Putin)
Authority that can force solutions

Propaganda is about controlling beliefs and behaviors. Propagandists use prejudice to create new beliefs, such as playing on aversion to certain delusions. Propaganda combines argumentation and activation of emotions such as fear, anger, guilt, and shame. When emotions and prejudices are activated, the purpose is to prevent reflection on premises and evidence. The latter is to ensure the intended outcome of false arguments. This becomes stronger when the propaganda is presented on several platforms, both within media and social media.

Facts and fictions

Facts and fiction are mixed in an ingenious way in propaganda. Often the most important thing is to create trust in the propagandist. Somewhat different instruments as means for influencing the population are used in the West and Ukraine than in Russia during the war in Ukraine. This can then facilitate distortions and misinformation that are perceived as credible by the recipient.

Propaganda downplays one`s own mistakes and blame and responsibility are passed on to others who are blamed. After Ukraine chose to say no to the peace agreement with Russia in April 2022, allegations of massacres, atrocities and war crimes in Bucha emerged. There is reason to question what happened in Bucha. Was what that was claimed true or was it propaganda created to demonize President Putin and the Russians?

Joseph Goebbels, Hitler-Germany`s Minister of Propaganda said: "If one only repeats an unfounded claim enough times, the people will eventually accept it as the truth". Today, we are constantly exposed to propaganda. It is often easy to believe what is said on TV and in the newspapers. Both television and newspapers can spread propaganda. If the propaganda is skillfully executed, it can be difficult to distinguish true from false. After Nine Eleven, intense lobbying led to the concept "Islam the Religion of peace". It obscured the religious element of the Nine Eleven attacks on the United States. The term entered Western societies without people thinking that it could be a constructed term,

The context of propaganda

Propaganda must be understood as propaganda, but also within the framework in which the propaganda has been developed. This is both about culture and means of propaganda that are either known or unknown in the respective societies. During the war in Ukraine much has been dismissed as Russian propaganda. I would say that as a resident of a Western country, I have a poorer ability for seeing through Russian propaganda than Western propaganda. Although Russian propaganda has several means in common with Western propaganda, there are also cultural differences. What seems like good propaganda in Russia does not have the same cultural prerequisites in Western countries. And vice versa.

Before former President Reagan visited Russia, he learned popular Russian expressions. It gave him a unique opportunity for communication. Few in the West bother to familiarize themselves with Russian culture. Therefore, several features of Russian culture- and propaganda – are inaccessible to people in the West. During the war, however, Western propaganda gained a far stronger impact than Russian propaganda.

During the war in Ukraine, propaganda is actively used to create an enemy image of President Putin, Russia, and Russians. Reasonable reporting from the war does not seem enough. The population in Western countries must also be convinced that it is a war in which the West is white, and that Russia is even blacker than the night. Propaganda never settles for the truth. Propaganda must convince more than the truth. To gain support for a cause of action or a war.

Propaganda will often rely on words and images that move people. Words and images that engage the emotions of the population. Although Norway is not directly affected by the war, questions about the war in Ukraine have enraged people. Even people who knew nothing about Ukraine. Also, pacifists have changed their minds during this war. Since 2022, even former pacifists have become in favor of sending weapons to Ukraine. Hardly anyone talks about dialogue.

When the propaganda meet reality

It has long been a great distance between the situation in Ukraine and what is reported in the mainstream media. Western media has become an important instrument for the propaganda of wars.

Politicians can ensure that propaganda is designed to create support for an issue. Unfortunately, many media outlets do not distinguish between facts and propaganda. It is also about strong commercial interests in the media, which often see themselves benefited by the population believing in the moral good of engaging in Ukraine.

The triplets of propaganda

In a way, propaganda is like the second triplet. Governments can use both legitimate, dubious, and legitimate reasons to create propaganda. While the governments are the ones who want propaganda in certain areas, they are dependent on that propaganda are both being made and distributed. Media plays an important role in bringing the propaganda to the global audience and in conveying propaganda to readers and viewers.

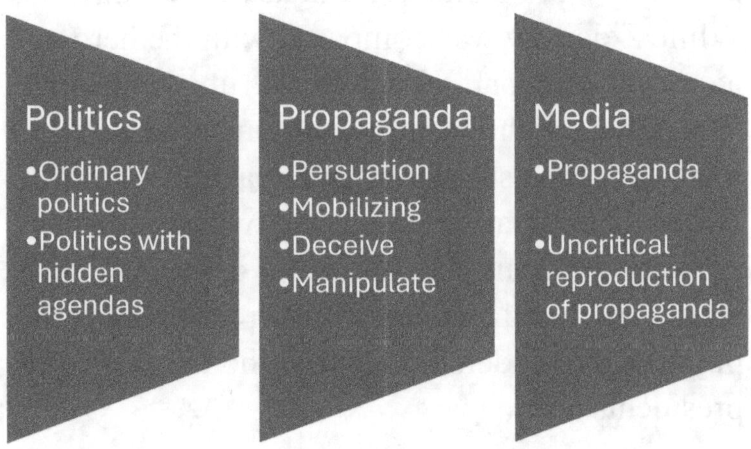

Fig.3 A model of propaganda, politics and media

Propaganda through narratives

The narrative has often become an important part of propaganda. Through narratives, propaganda uses the narrative to influence. During the war in Ukraine there is a battle over the narrative of the war. The propaganda is very cleverly made in the West. Many tools are used to create a convincing narrative about the war. Stories have been created about the war and scare images are created about the dangers if Russia is winning the war in Ukraine. In the beginning of the war in 2022, it was about President Zelensky as the good guy and President Putin as the bad guy. While Zelensky was compared with the hero and icon of the Second World War, Prime Minister Winston Churchill, Putin was compared to gangsters, fascists, Peter the Great and Adolf Hitler. The narratives about the two presidents are very different, like night and day, black and white, and good and evil. This in turn affects the population's understanding of who the two presidents are.

A clash in communication?

The question is also whether and when propaganda can cause a breakdown in communication. After more than two years of war, the propaganda is still very effective. However, President Zelensky has gradually lost his status, but the West still insists that President Putin is a terrible leader. Seen in light of the war in Ukraine, the image of the aggressor, it may be a reasonable point of view, but the demonization began before the war in Ukraine. This in turn has both blocked and legitimized the neglect of necessary communication about the war, and what may have been the wisest paths to peace. Propaganda can compete with the most dangerous weapons in a war. At the same time, it can contribute to the breakdown of communication – a clash of communication, due to propaganda.

Summary

Propaganda is a powerful tool. It can influence and manipulate the population. The war in Ukraine has undoubtedly also been fought in the media and social media. Wars are also and always battles for the truth – the truth in the opinion. Western propaganda undoubtedly won the propaganda war in the first two years after the start of the war in 2022.The narrative that said Zelensky was a hero and Putin was everything that could be wrong, had a great impact on the opinion in Western countries. During the ear, people have been able to see through the media that President Zelensky is not a hero. Nevertheless, the story of the hero still sits in many people`s mind.

Putin`s speech in Munich in 2007

Introduction

The speech President Putin gave during the security conference in Munich in 2007 implied a difference in the West`s attitude towards President Putin and Russia. In the Western media, one could read that President Putin was seething with rage and showed his true face in Munich.

In this chapter I will analyze Putin`s speech. It will also be published since it is so important. I will also look at how President Putin emphasizes rhetoric in his communication with the public at the security conference in Munich.

What does the speech actually say?

When I translated the speech into Norwegian in 2022, I became confused in relation to both the text and my understanding of it. What I had read about the speech did not match with the text that I read. I asked myself several times during the autumn of 2022 if there was something that I did not understand in the speech. My doubt about my own judgment in the interpretation of the speech was probably about what psychologists call cognitive dissonance, when there are discrepancies between different truths that are presented to you. I had trouble understanding that the speech was so provocative that it dramatically changed the climate between the West and Russia. I did not find the speech provocative. President Putin criticized the United States for monopolistic dominance in international relation. It was a legitimate position on international politics. Of course, it went against the American understanding of who is who on the global chessboard. In this sense, the speech was a violation of the Americans' right to define the world, as if they ruled over the entire global chessboard. Putin`s speech was therefore a kick to the Americans 'understanding of the world. The speech did not show the respect the Americans took for granted.

After the end of the Second World War the United States had been accustomed to being the world`s most important superpower. Before the dissolution of the Soviet Union in 1991, this was balanced by the importance and power of the former Soviet Union. From 1991 it was a unipolar world. It was in the Americans' interest that it continued like this. It is within this perspective that we must interpret the rage against Putin`s speech in Munich. He simply did not show Americans the humility they took for granted.

The speech at the Munich Conference on Security policy

"Thank you very much Madam Federal Chancellor, Mr Teltschik, ladies and gentlemen!

I am truly grateful to be invited to such a representative conference that has assembled politicians, military officials, entrepreneurs and experts from more than 40 nations.

This conference`s structure allows me to avoid excessive politeness and the need to speak in roundabout, pleasant but empty diplomatic terms. This conference`s format will allow me to say what I really think about international security problems. And if my comments seem unduly polemical, pointed or inexact to our colleagues, the I would ask you not to get angry with me. After all, this is only a conference. And I hope that after the first two or three minutes of my speech Mr Teltschik will not turn on the red light over there.

Therefore. It is well known that international security comprises much more than issues relating to military and political stability. It involves the stability of the global economy, overcoming poverty, economic security and developing a dialogue between civilizations.

This universal, indivisible character of security is expressed as the basic principle that "security for one is security for all". As Franklin D. Roosevelt said during the first few days that the Second World War was breaking out:" When peace has been broken anywhere, the peace of all countries everywhere is in danger."

These words remain topical today. Incidentally, the theme of our conference- global crisis, global responsibility – exemplifies this.

Only two decades ago the world was ideologically divided, and it was the huge strategic potential of two superpowers that ensured global security.

This global stand-off pushed the sharpest economic and social problems to the margins of the international community`s and the world`s agenda. And, just like any war, the Cold War left us with live ammunition, figuratively speaking. I am referring to ideological stereotypes, double standards and other typical aspects of Cold War bloc thinking.

The unipolar world that had been proposed after the Cold War did not take place either.

The history of humanity certainly has gone through unipolar periods and seen aspirations to world supremacy. And what hasn`t happened in world history?

However, what is a unipolar world? However, one might embellish this term, at the end of the day it refers to one type of situation, namely one centre of authority, one centre of force, one centre of decision-making.

It is a world in which there is one master, one sovereign. And at the end of the day this is pernicious not only for all those within this system, but also for the sovereign itself because it destroys itself from within.

And this certainly has nothing in common with democracy. Because, as you know, democracy is the power of the majority in light of the interests and opinions of the minority.

Incidentally, Russia – we- are constantly being taught about democracy. But for some reason those who teach us do not want to learn themselves.

I consider that the unipolar model is not only unacceptable but also impossible in today`s world. And this is not only because if there was individual leadership in today`s- and precisely in today`s- world, then the military, political and economic resources would not suffice. What is even more important is that the model itself is flawed because at its basis there is and can be no moral foundations for modern civilization.

Along with this, what is happening in today`s world – and we just started to discuss this – is a tentative to introduce precisely this concept into international affairs, the concept of a unipolar world.

And with which results?

Unilateral and frequently illegitimate actions have not resolved any problems. Moreover, they have caused new human tragedies and created new centres of tension. Judge for yourselves: wars as well as local and regional conflicts have not diminished. Mer Teltschik mentioned this very gently. And no less people perish in these conflicts – even more are dying than before. Significantly more, significantly more!

Today we are witnessing an almost uncontained hyper use of force – military force- in international relations, force that is plunging the world into an abyss of permanent conflicts. As a result we do not have sufficient strength to find a comprehensive solution to any one of these conflicts. Finding a political settlement also becomes impossible.

We are seeing a greater and greater disdain for the basic principles of international law. And independent legal norms are, as a matter of fact, coming closer to one state`s legal system. One state and, of course, first and foremost the United States has overstepped its national borders in every way. This is visible in the economic, political, cultural and educational policies it imposes on other nations. Well, who likes this? Who is happy about this?

In international relations we increasingly see the desire to resolve a given question according to so-called issues of political expediency, based on current political climate.

And of course this extremely dangerous. It results in the fact that no one feels safe. I want to emphasise this-no one feels safe! Because no one can feel that international law is like a stone that will protect them. Of course such a policy stimulates an arms race.

The force`s dominance inevitably encourages a number of countries to acquire weapons of mass destruction. Moreover, significantly new threats – though they were also well-known before- have appeared, and today threats such as terrorism have taken a global character.

I am convinced that we have reached the decisive moment when we must seriously think about the architecture of global security.

And we must proceed by searching for a reasonable balance between the interests of all participants in the international dialogue. Especially since the international landscape is so varied and changes so quickly – changes in light of the dynamic development in a whole number of countries and regions.

Madam Federal Chancellor already mentioned this. The combined GDP measured in purchasing power parity of countries such as India and China are already greater than that of the United States. And a similar calculation with the GDP of the BRIC countries- Brazil, Russia. India and China – surpasses the cumulative GDP of the EU. And according to experts this gap will only increase in the future.

There is no reason to doubt that the economic potential of the new centres of global economic growth will inevitably be converted into political influence and will strengthen multipolarity.

In connection with this the role of multilateral diplomacy is significantly increasing. The need for principles such as openness, transparency and predictability in politics is uncontested and the use of force should be a really exceptional measure, comparable to using the death penalty in the judicial systems of certain states.

However, today we are witnessing the opposite tendency, namely a situation in which countries that forbid the death penalty even for murderers and other, dangerous criminals are airily participating in military operations that are difficult to consider legitimate. And as a matter of fact, these conflicts are killing people – hundreds and thousands of civilians!

But at the same time the question arises of whether we should be indifferent and aloof to various internal conflicts inside countries, to authoritarian regimes, to tyrants, and to the proliferation of weapons of mass destruction? As a matter of fact, this was also at the centre of the question that our dear colleague Mr Liberman asked the Federal Chancellor. If I correctly understood your question (addressing Mr Lieberman), then of course it is a serious one!

Can we be indifferent observers in view of what is happening? I will try to answer your question as well: of course not.

But do we have the means to counter these threats? Certainly we do. It is sufficient to look at recent history. Did not our country have a peaceful transition to democracy? Indeed, we witnessed a peaceful transformation of the Soviet regime – a peaceful transformation! And what a regime! With what a number of weapons, including nuclear weapons! Why should we start bombing and shooting now at every available opportunity? Is it the case when without the threat of mutual destruction we do not have enough political culture, respect for democratic values and for the law.

I am convinced that the only mechanism that can make decisions about using military force as a last resort is the Charter of the United Nations. And in connection with this, either I did not understand what our colleague, the Italian Defence Minister, just said or what he said was inexact. In any case, I understood that the use of force can only be legitimate when the decision is taken by NATO, the EU, or the UN. If he really does think so, then we have different points of view. Or I didn`t hear correctly. The use of force can only be considered legitimate if the decision is sanctioned by the UN. And we do not need to substitute NATO or the EU for the UN. When the UN will truly unite the forces of the international community and can really react to events in various countries, when we will leave behind this disdain for international law, then the situation will be able to change. Otherwise the situation will simply result in a dead end, and the number of serious mistakes will be multiplied. Along with this, it is necessary to make sure that international law have a universal character both in the conception and application of its norms.

And one must not forget that democratic political actions necessarily go along with discussion and a laborious decision-making process.

Dear ladies and gentlemen!

The potential danger of destabilization of international relations is connected with obvious stagnation in the disarmament issue.

Russia supports the renewal of dialogue on this important question.

It is important to conserve the international legal framework relating to weapons destruction and therefore ensure continuity in the process of reducing nuclear weapons.

Together with the United States of America we agreed to reduce our nuclear strategic missile capabilities to up to 1700-2000 nuclear warheads by 31 December 2012. Russia intends to strictly fulfil the obligations it has taken on. We hope that our partners will also act in a transparent way and will refrain from laying aside a couple of hundreds superfluous nuclear warheads for a rainy day. And if today the new American Defence Minister declares that the United States will not hide these superfluous weapons in warehouse or, as one might say, under a pillow or under the blanket, then I suggest that we all rise and greet this declaration standing. It would be a very important declaration.

Russia strictly adheres to and intends to further adhere to the Treaty on the Non-Proliferation of Nuclear Weapons as well as the multilateral supervision regime for missile technologies. The principles incorporated in these documents are universal ones.

In connection with this I would like to recall that in the 1980s the USSR and the United States signed an agreement on destroying a whole range of small-and medium-range missiles but these documents do not have a universal character.

Today many other countries have these missiles, including the Democratic People's Republic of Korea, the Republic of Korea, India, Iran, Pakistan and Israel. Many countries are working on these systems and plan to incorporate them as a part of their weapons arsenals. And only the United States and Russia bear the responsibility to no create such weapons systems.

It is obvious that in these conditions we must think about ensuring our own security.

At the same time, it is impossible to sanction the appearance of new, destabilising high-tech weapons. Needless to say it refers to measures to prevent a new area of confrontation, especially in outer space. Star wars is no longer a fantasy – it is a reality. In the middle of the 1980s our American partners were already able to intercept their own satellite.

In Russia`s opinion, the militarisation of outer space could have unpredictable consequences for the international community and provoke nothing less than the beginning of a nuclear era. And we have come forward more than once with initiatives designed to prevent the use of weapons in outer space.

Today I would like to tell you that we have prepared a project for an agreement on the prevention of deploying weapons in outer space. And in the near future it will be sent to our partners as an official proposal. Let's work on this together.

Plans to expand certain elements of the anti-missile defence system to Europe cannot help but disturb us. Who needs the next step of what would be, in this case, an inevitable arms race? I deeply doubt that Europeans themselves do.

Missile weapons with a range of about five to eight thousand kilometres that really pose a threat to Europe do not exist in any of the so-called problem countries. And in the near future and prospects, this will not happen and is not even foreseeable. And any hypothetical launch of, for example, a North Korean rocket to American territory through western Europe obviously contradicts the laws for ballistic. As we say in Russia, it would be like using the right hand to reach the left ear.

And here in Germany I cannot help but mention the pitiable condition of the Treaty on Conventional Armed Forces in Europe.

The Adapted treaty on Conventional Armed Forces in Europe was signed in 1999. It took into account a new geopolitical reality, namely the elimination of the Warsaw bloc. Seven years have passed and only four states have ratified this document, including the Russian Federation.

NATO countries openly declared that they will not ratify this treaty, including the provisions on flank restrictions (on deploying a certain number of armed forces in the flank zones), until Russia removed its military bases from Georgia and Moldova. Our army is leaving Georgia, even according to an accelerated schedule. We resolved the problems we had with our Georgian colleagues, as everybody knows. There a still 1,500 servicemen in Moldova that are carrying out peacekeeping operations and protecting warehouses with ammunition left over from Soviet times. We constantly discuss the issue with Mr Solana and he knows our position. We are ready to further work in this direction.

But what is happening at the same time? Simultaneously the so-called flexible frontline American bases with up to five thousand men in each. It turns out that NATO puts its frontline forces on our borders, and we continue to strictly fulfil the treaty obligations and do not react to these actions at all.

I think it is obvious that NATO expansion does not have any relation with the modernization of the Alliance itself or with ensuring security in Europe. On the contrary, it represents a serious provocation that reduces the level of mutual trust. And we have the right to ask: against whom is this expansion intended? And what happened to the assurances our western partners made after the dissolution of the Warsaw Pact? Where are those declarations today? No one even remembers them. But I will allow myself to remind this audience what was said. I would like to quote the speech NATO General Secretary Mr

Wörner in Brussels on 17 May 1990. He said at the time that: "the fact that we are ready not to place a NATO army outside of German territory gives the Soviet Union a firm security guarantee". Where are these guarantees?

The stones and concrete blocks of the Berlin Wall have long been distributed as souvenirs. But we should not forget that the fall of the Berlin Wall was possible thanks to a historic choice – one that was also made by our people, the people of Russia – a choice in favour of democracy, freedom, openness, and a sincere partnership with all the members of the big European family.

And now they are trying to impose new dividing lines and walls on us – these walls may be virtual but they are nevertheless dividing, ones that cut through our continent. And is it possible that we will once again require many years and decades, as well as several generations of politicians, to dissemble and dismantle these new walls?

Dear ladies and gentlemen!

We are unequivocally in favour of strengthening the regime of non- proliferation. The present international legal principles allow us to develop technologies to manufacture nuclear fuel for peaceful purposes. And many countries with all good reasons want to create their own nuclear energy as a basis for their energy independence. But we also understand that these technologies can be quickly transformed into nuclear weapons.

This creates serious international tensions. The situation surrounding the Iranian nuclear programme acts as a clear example. And if the international community does not find a reasonable solution for resolving this conflict of interests, the world will continue to suffer similar, destabilising crises because there are more threshold countries than simply Iran. We both know this. We are going to constantly fight against the threat of the proliferation of weapons of mass destruction.

Last year Russia put forward the initiative to establish international centres for the enrichment of uranium. We are open to the possibility that such centres not only be created in Russia, but also in countries where there is a legitimate basis for using civil nuclear energy. Countries that want to develop their nuclear energy could guarantee that they will receive fuel through direct participation in these centres. And the centres would, of course, operate under strict IAEA supervision.

The latest initiatives put forward by American President George W. Bush are in conformity with the Russian proposals. I consider that Russia and the USA are objectively and equally interested in strengthening the regime of the non- proliferation of weapons of mass destruction and their deployment. It is precisely our countries, with leading nuclear and missile capabilities, that must act as leaders in developing new, stricter non-proliferation measures. Russia is ready for such work. We are engaged in consultation with our American friends.

In general, we should talk about establishing a whole system of political incentives and economic stimuli whereby it would not be in states`interests to establish their own capabilities in the nuclear fuel cycle but they would still have the opportunity to develop nuclear energy and strengthen their energy capabilities.

In connection with this I shall talk about international energy cooperation in more detail. Madam Federal Chancellor also spoke about this briefly – she mentioned, touched on this theme. In the energy sector Russia intends to create uniform market principles and transparent conditions for all. It is obvious that energy prices must be determined by the market instead of being the subject of political speculation, economic pressure or blackmail.

We are open to cooperation. Foreign companies participate in all our major energy projects. According to different estimates, up to 26 percent of the oil extraction in Russia – and please think about this figure – up 26 percent of the oil extraction in Russia is done by foreign capital. Try, try to find me a similar example where Russian business participates extensively in key economic sectors in western countries. Such examples do not exist! There are not such examples.

I would also recall the parity of foreign investment in Russia and those Russia makes abroad. The parity is about fifteen to one. And here you have and obvious example of the openness and stability of the Russian economy.

Economic security is the sector in which all must adhere to uniform principles. We are ready to compete fairly.

For that reason more and more opportunities are appearing in the Russian economy. Experts and our western partners are objectively evaluating these changes. As such, Russia`s OECD sovereign credit rating improved and Russia passed from the fourth to the third group. And today in Munich I would like to use this occasion to thank German colleagues for their help in the above decision.

Furthermore. As you know, the process of Russia joining the WTO has reached its final stages. I would point out that during long, difficult talks we heard words about freedom of speech, free trade, and equal possibilities more than once but, for some reason, exclusively in reference to the Russian market.

And there is still one more important theme that directly affects global security. Today many talk about the struggle against poverty. What is actually happening in this sphere? On the one hand, financial resources are allocated for programmes to help the world's poorest countries – and at times substantial financial resources. But to be honest, and many here know this- linked with the development of that same donor country`s companies. And on the other hand, developed countries simultaneously keep their agricultural subsidies and limit some countries` access to high-tech products.

And let`s say things as they are – one hand distributes charitable help and the other hand not only preserves economic backwardness but also reaps the profits thereof. The increasing social tension in depressed regions inevitably results in the growth of radicalism, extremism, feeds terrorism and local conflicts. And if all this happens in, shall we say, a region such as the Middle East where there is increasingly the sense that the world at large is unfair, then there is the risk of global destabilization.

It is obvious that the world`s leading countries should see this threat. And that they should therefore build a more democratic, fairer system of global economic relations, a system that would give everyone the chance and the possibility to develop.

Dear ladies and gentlemen, speaking at the Conference in Security Policy, it is impossible not to mention the activities of the Organisation for Security and Cooperation in Europe (OSCE). As is well-known, this organisation was created to examine all – I shall emphasise this- all aspects of security: military, political, economic, humanitarian and, especially, the relation between these spheres.

What do we see happening today? We see that this balance is clearly destroyed. People are trying to transform the OSCE into a vulgar instrument designed to promote the foreign policy interests of one or a group of countries. And this task is also being accomplished by the OSCE`s bureaucratic apparatus which is absolutely not connected with the state founders in any way. Decision-making procedures and the involvement of so-called non-governmental organisations are tailored for this task. These organisations are formally independent, but they are purposefully financed and therefore under control.

According to the founding documents, in the humanitarian sphere the OSCE is designed to assist country members in observing international human rights norms at their request. This is an important task. We support this. But this does not mean interfering in the internal affairs of other countries, and especially not imposing a regime that determines how these states should live and develop.

It is obvious that such interference does not promote the development of democratic states at all. On the contrary, it makes them dependent and, as a consequence, politically and economically unstable.

We expect that the OSCE be guided by its primary tasks and build relations with sovereign states based on respect, trust and transparency.

Dear ladies and gentlemen!

In conclusion I would like to note the following. We very often- and personally, I very often – hear appeals by our partners, including European partners, to the effect that Russia should play an increasingly active role in world affairs.

In connection with this I would allow myself to make one small remark. It is hardly necessary to incite us to do so. Russia is a country with a history that spans more than a thousand years, and has practically always used the privilege to carry out an independent foreign policy.

We are not going to change this tradition today. At the same time, we are well aware of how the world has changed and we have a realistic sense of our own opportunities and potential. And of course we would like to interact with responsible and independent partners with whom we could work together in constructing a fair and democratic world order that would ensure security and prosperity not only for a select few, but for all.

Thank you for your attention."

What does the speech convey?

President Putin gave a speech with several strong messages. It is a speech characterized by a president who wants to convey much of how he perceives the world and what the situation is for power and democracy in the world. The speech is deeply serious. There are no superfluous words. If the speech were a human, it would not have a single extra gram of fat. The speech is logical, strong, and factual. It is also understandable that it provoked reactions. It was as if, with his speech, Putin threw a stone right into the heart of the Western self-image. Figuratively speaking.

The beginning of the speech

President Putin clearly knew that the speech would provoke the audience in Munich. He therefore begins with reservations and humility. In rhetoric *benevolus* is an expression for kind, friendly and favorable. Putin`s starting point was that he was among friends. He asked for understanding of what he was going to say. He almost warned the audience with a friendly introduction.

At the beginning of the speech, he quotes the words of former US President, Franklin D. Roosevelt: "When peace has broken anywhere, the peace of all countries everywhere is in danger." With this quote, Putin shows both knowledge of the United States, but also the nature of war. And that war in one place can lead to war in several places.

The message in the speech

If the speech had been given by the son in the family, the speech could have been about the brother both having taken the entire inheritance while saying he even was better than the brother who received nothing of the inheritance. This is, of course, figuratively speaking, but it is also a picture that sums up President Putin`s anger and wishes for developments in international relations, disarmament, economic cooperation, and binding agreements.

After the introductory words, President Putin almost introduces a model for the content of the speech. He says that international security is about more than military and political stability. He refers to the fight against poverty, economic security, and the importance of dialogue.

It is understandable that the United States reacted to Putin`s attack on the unipolar world order. This has been the privilege of Americans since the fall of the Berlin Wall. What Putin says in the speech, however, is nearly the same as what many politicians on the left in Europe have been saying for decades. The message should not have been unknown to the US.

It was unnecessary to react with rage and contempt, but it was at the same time deeply human. Putin`s speech was like a rhetorical sword clow to the solar plexus of the American body.

After the wars of aggression in Afghanistan and Iraq, the United States was really in a glass house morally speaking. The war in Iraq was based on lies about weapons of mass destruction. The war was a disaster for Iraq, but also for the American self- image. When Putin gave the speech in Munich, the two failed wars in Iraq and Afghanistan were still going on.

The speech as rhetoric

President Putin shows that he values words in what he writes and speaks. Except for the introduction of the speech, there is a total absence of formulations that can appeal to the positive emotions in the audience. The speech is strictly logical. It sticks strictly to what Putin wants to convey. Every sentence is well thought out. The language is economical and clear. Putin has a way of speaking that shows that he emphasizes facts and views more than fluency in the speech. Putin seeks to influence with arguments, the logos of rhetoric, rather than the many other means of rhetoric.

President Putin and his speech	*The audience in Munich*
A speech characterized by the logos of rhetoric	The cultural hegemony in the West as a collective culture in the audience Cultural arrogance Prejudices against Russia Prejudices against President Putin

Fig 4.A model of Putin and the audience in Munich

Absence of rhetorical devices

There is an old saying that the speaker never can take the attention of the audience for granted. Except for the introduction, Putin delivered a brutally honest speech in Munich. It was a very important speech, but he did not reach the audience. Nor did he use rhetorical tricks to get the audience to see the issues from Russia`s perspective, from Putin`s perspective.

Summary

President Putin gave probably the most important speech in the new millennium in Munich. The speech was factual from the beginning to the end. Putin began with the *benevolus* of rhetoric. There he signaled humility and asked for understanding for what he was going to say. After the introduction, the speech was factual down to the smallest detail. Putin gave the speech in the logos of rhetoric.

Even if Putin`s speech is one of the most important speeches after the beginning of a new millennium, the audience was hardly interested in what Putin had to say. In the years since, however, both the speech and Putin have been demonized. I feel sad thinking of the cultural arrogance with which this speech was met. It could have been a good starting point for a constructive dialogue between Russia and the West. The failure was due to both Putin`s inability to influence the public, but also the public`s unwillingness to listen and be influenced by the important speech.

Speech February 24,2022

Introduction

President Putin gave a speech on February 24, 2022, in which he gave a rationale for the invasion of Ukraine. This is a historically important speech. It also shows that the war has changed from its original goal stated in this speech. The speech is therefore an important document to understand both why Russia invaded Ukraine, but also how the role of the West contributed to change the goals of the war.

The speech

Here is a reproduction of most of the speech:

"Citizens of Russia, friends,

I consider it necessary today to speak again about the tragic events in Donbass and the key aspects of ensuring the security of Russia.

I will begin with what I said in my address on February 21,2022. I spoke about our biggest concerns and worries, and about the fundamental threats which irresponsible Western politicians created for Russia consistently, rudely and unceremoniously from year to year. I am referring to the eastward expansion of NATO, which is moving its military infrastructure ever closer to the Russian border.

It is a fact that over the past 30 years we have been patiently trying to come to an agreement with the leading NATO countries regarding the principles of equal and indivisible security in Europe. In response to our proposals, we invariably faced either cynical deception and lies or attempts at pressure and blackmail, while the North Atlantic alliance continued to expand despite our protest and concerns. Its military machine is moving and, as I said, is approaching our very border.

Why is this happening? Where did this insolent manner of talking down from the height of their exceptionalism, infallibility and all-permissiveness come from? What is the explanation for this contemptuous and disdainful attitude to our interests and absolutely legitimate demands?

The answer is simple. Everything is clear and obvious. In the late 1980s, the Soviet Union grew weaker and subsequently broke apart. That experience should serve as a good lesson for us, because it has shown us that the paralysis of power and will is the step towards complete degradation and oblivion. We lost confidence for only one moment, but it was enough to disrupt the balance of forces in the world.

As a result, the old treaties and agreements are no longer effective. Entreaties and requests do not help. Anything that does not suite the dominant state, the powers that be, is denounced as archaic, obsolete and useless. At the same time, everything it regards as useful is presented as the ultimate truth and forced on others regardless of the cost, abusively and by any means available. Those who refuse to comply are subjected to strong -arm tactics.

What I am saying now does not concerns only Russia, and Russia is not the only country that is worried about this. This has to do with the entire system of international relations, and sometimes even US allies. The collapse of the Soviet Union led to a redivision of the world, and the norms of international law that developed by that time - and the most important of them, the fundamental norms that were adopted following WW2 and largely formalized its outcome – came in the way of those who declared themselves the winners of the Cold War.

Of course, practice, international relations and the rules regulating them had to take into account the changes that took place in the world and in the balance of forces. However, this should have been done professionally, smoothly, patiently, and with due regard and respect for the interests of all states and one`s own responsibility. Instead, we saw a state of euphoria created by the feeling of absolute superiority, a kind of modern absolutism, coupled with the low cultural standards and arrogance of those who formulated and pushed through decisions that suited only themselves. The situation took a different turn.

There are many examples of this. First a bloody military operation was waged against Belgrade, without the UN Security Council`s sanction but with aircraft and missiles used in the heart of Europe. The bombing of peaceful cities and vital infrastructure went on for several weeks. I have to recall these facts, because some Western colleagues prefer to forget them, and when we mentioned the event, they prefer to avoid speaking about international law, instead emphasizing the circumstances which they interpret as they think necessary.

Then came the turn of Iraq, Libya and Syria. The illegal use of military power against Libya and the distortion of all the UN Security Council decisions on Libya ruined the state, created a huge seat of international terrorism, and pushed the country towards a humanitarian catastrophe, into the vortex of civil war, which has continued there for years. The tragedy, which was created for hundreds of thousands and even millions of people not only in Libya but in the whole region, has led to a large-scale exodus from the Middle East and North Africa to Europe.

A similar fate was also prepared for Syria. The combat operations conducted by the Western coalition in that country without the Syrian government`s approval or the UN Security

Council's sanction can only be defined as aggression and intervention.

But the example that stands apart from the above events is, of course, the invasion of Iraq without any legal grounds. They used the pretext of allegedly reliable information available in the United States about the presence of weapons of mass destruction in Iraq. To prove that allegation, the US Secretary of State held up a vial with white powder, publicly for the whole world to see, assuring the international community that it was a chemical warfare agent created in Iraq. It later turned out that all of that was fake and a sham, and that Iraq did not have any chemical weapons. Incredible and shocking but true. We witnessed lies made at the highest state level and voiced from the UN rostrum. As a result we see a tremendous loss in human life, damage, destruction, and a colossal upsurge of terrorism.

Overall, it appears that nearly everywhere, in many regions of the world where the United States brought its law and order, this created bloody, non-healing wounds and the curse of international terrorism and extremism. I have only mentioned the most glaring but far from only examples of disregard of international law.

This array includes promises not to expand NATO eastwards even by an inch, To reiterate: they have deceived us, or, to put it simply, they have played us. Sure, one often hears that politics is a dirty business. It could be, but it shouldn't be as dirty as it is now, not to such an extent. This type of con-artist behavior is contrary not only to the principles of international relations but also and above all to the generally accepted norms of morality and ethics. Where is justice and truth here? Just lies and hypocrisy all around.

Incidentally, US politicians, political scientists and journalists write and say that a veritable "empire of lies" has been created inside the United States in recent years. It is hard to disagree with this- it is really so. But one should not be modest about it: the United States is still a great country and a system-forming power. All its satellites not only humbly and obediently say yes to and parrot it at the slightest pretext but also imitate its behavior and enthusiastically accept the rules it is offering them. Therefore, one can say with good reason and confidence that the whole so-called Western bloc formed by the United States in its own image and likeness is, in its entirety, the same "empire of lies."

As for our country, after the disintegration of the USSR, given the entire unprecedented openness of the new, modern Russia, its readiness to work honestly with the United States and other Western partners, and its practically unilateral disarmament, they immediately tried to put the final squeeze on us, finish us off, and utterly destroy us. This is how it was in the 1990s and the early 2000s, when the so-called collective West was actively supporting separatism and gangs of mercenaries in southern Russia. What victims, what losses we had to sustain and what trials we had to go through at that time before we broke the back of international terrorism in the Caucasus! We remember this and will never forget.

Properly speaking, the attempts to use us in their own interests never ceased until quite recently: they sought to destroy our traditional values and force on us their false values that would erode us, our people from within, the attitudes they have been aggressively imposing on their countries, attitudes that are directly leading to degradation and degeneration, because they are contrary to human nature. This is not going to happen. No one has ever succeeded in doing this, nor will they succeed now.

Despite all that, in December 2021, we made yet another attempt to reach agreement with the United States and its allies on the principles of European security and NATO`s non-expansion. Our efforts were in vain. The United States has not changed its position. It does not believe it necessary to agree with Russia on a matter critical for us. The United States is pursuing its own objectives, while neglecting our interests.

Of course, this situation begs a question: what next, what are we to expect? If history is any guide, we know that in 1940 and early 1941 the Soviet Union went to great lengths to prevent war or at least delay its outbreak. To this end, the USSR sought not to provoke the potential aggressor until the very end by refraining or postponing the most urgent and obvious preparations it had to make to defend itself from an imminent attack. When it finally acted, it was too late.

As a result, the country was not prepared to counter the invasion by Nazi Germany, which attacked our Motherland on June 22,1941, without declaring war. The country stopped the enemy and went on to defeat it, but this came at a tremendous cost. The attempt to appease the aggressor ahead of the Great Patriotic War proved to be a mistake which came at a high cost for our people. In the first months after the hostilities broke out, we lost vast territories of strategic importance, as well as millions of lives. We will not make this mistake the second time. We have no right to do so.

Those who aspire to global dominance have publicly designated Russia as their enemy. They did so with impunity. Make no mistake, they had no reason to act this way. It is true that they have considerable financial, scientific, technological, and military capabilities. We are aware of this and have an objective view of the economic threats we have been hearing, just as our ability to counter this brash and never-ending blackmail. Let me reiterate that we have no illusions in the regard and are extremely realistic in our assessments.

As for military affairs, even after the dissolution of the USSR and losing a considerable part of its capabilities, today`s Russia remains one of the most powerful nuclear states. Moreover, it has certain advantage in several cutting-edge weapons. In this context, there should be no doubt for anyone that any potential aggressor will face defeat and ominous consequences should it directly attack our country.

At the same time, technology, including in the defence sector, is changing rapidly. One day there is one leader, and tomorrow another, but a military presence in territories bordering on Russia, if we permit it to go ahead, will stay for decades to come or maybe forever, creating and ever mounting and totally unacceptable threat for Russia.

Even now, with NATO`s eastward expansion the situation for Russia has been becoming worse and more dangerous by the year. Moreover, these past days NATO leadership has been blunt in its statement that they need to accelerate and step up efforts to bring the alliance`s infrastructure closer to Russia`s borders. In other words, they have been toughening their position. We cannot stay idle and passively observe these developments. This would be an absolutely irresponsible thing to do for us.

Any further expansion of the North Atlantic alliance`s infrastructure or the ongoing efforts to gain a military foothold of the Ukrainian territory are unacceptable for us. Of course, the question is not about NATO itself. It merely serves as a tool of US foreign policy. The problem is that in territories adjacent to Russia, which I have to note is our historical land, a hostile "anti-Russia" is taking shape. Fully controlled from the outside, it is doing everything to attract NATO armed forces and obtain cutting-edge weapons.

For the United States and its allies, it is a policy of containing Russia, with obvious geopolitical dividend. For our country, it is a matter of life and death, a matter of our historical future as a nation. This is not an exaggeration; this is a fact. It is not only a very real threat to our interests but to the very existence of our state and to its sovereignty. It is the red line which we have spoken about on numerous occasions. They have crossed it.

This brings me to the situation in Donbass. We can see that the forces that staged the coup in Ukraine in 2014 have seized power, are keeping it with the help of ornamental election procedures and have abandoned the path of peaceful conflict settlement. For eight years, for eight endless years we have been doing everything possible to settle the situation by peaceful political means. Everything was in vain.

As I said in my previous address, you cannot look without compassion at what is happening there. It became impossible to tolerate it. We had to stop that atrocity, that genocide of the millions of people who live there and who pinned their hopes on Russia, on all of us. It is their aspirations, the feelings and pain of these people that were the main motivating force behind our decision to recognize the independence of the Donbass people`s republics.

I would like to additionally emphasise the following. Focused on their own goals, the leading NATO countries are supporting the far-right nationalists and neo- Nazis in Ukraine, those who will never forgive the people of

Crimea and Sevastopol for freely making a choice to reunite with Russia.

They will undoubtedly try to bring war to Crimea just as they have done in Donbass, to kill innocent people, just as members of the punitive units of Ukrainian nationalists and Hitler's accomplices did during the Great Patriotic War. The have also openly laid claim to several other Russian regions.

If we look at the sequence of events and the incoming reports, the showdown between Russia and these forces cannot be avoided. It is only a matter of time. They are getting ready and waiting for the right moment. Moreover, they went as far as aspire to acquire nuclear weapons. We will not let this happen.

I have already said that Russia accepted the new geopolitical reality after the dissolution of the USSR, we have been treating all new post-Soviet states with respect and will continue to act this way. We respect and will respect their sovereignty, as proven by the assistance we provided to Kazakhstan when it faced tragic events and a challenge in terms of its statehood and integrity. However, Russia cannot feel safe, develop, and exist while facing a permanent threat from the territory of today`s Ukraine.

Let me remind you that in 2000-2005 we used our military to push back against terrorists in the Caucasus and stood up for the integrity of our state. We preserved Russia. In 2014, we supported the people of Crimea and Sevastopol. In 2015, we used our Armed Forces to create a reliable shield that prevented terrorists from Syria from penetrating Russia. This was a matter of defending ourselves. We had no other choice.

The same is happening today. They did not leave us any other option for defending Russia and our people, other than the one we are forced to use today. In these circumstances, we have to take bold and immediate action. The people`s republic of Donbass have asked Russia for help.

In this context, in accordance with Article 51(Chapter 7) in the UN Charter, with permission of Russia`s Federation Council, and in execution of the treaties of friendship and mutual assistance with the Donets People`s Republic and the Lugansk People`s Republic, ratified by the Federal Assembly on February 22, I made a decision to carry out a special military operation.

The purpose of this operation is to protect people who for eight years now, have been facing humiliation and genocide perpetrated by the Kiev regime. To this end, we will seek to demilitarize and denazify Ukraine, as well as bring to trial those who perpetrated numerous bloody crimes against civilians, including against citizens of the Russian Federation.

It is not our plan to occupy the Ukrainian territory. We do not intend to impose anything on anyone by force. At the same time, we have been hearing an increasing number of statements coming from the West that there is no need any more to abide by the documents setting forth the outcomes of World War 2, as signed by the totalitarian Soviet regime. How can we respond to that?

The outcomes of World War 2 and the sacrifices our people had to make to defeat Nazism are sacred. This does not contradict the high values of human rights and freedoms in the reality that emerged over the post-war decades. This does not mean that nations cannot enjoy the right to self- determination, which is enshrined in Article 1 of the UN Charter.

Let me remind you that the people living in the territories which are part of today`s Ukraine were not asked how they want to build their lives when the USSR was created or after Word War 2. Freedom guides our policy, the freedom to choose independently our future and the future of our children. We believe that all the peoples living in today`s Ukraine, anyone who want to do this, must be able to enjoy the rights to make a free choice.

In this context I would like to address the citizens of Ukraine. In 2014, Russia was obliged to protect the people of Crimea and Sevastopol from those yourself call "nats". The people of Crimea and Sevastopol made their choice in favour of being with their historical homeland, Russia, and we supported their choice. As I said, we could not act otherwise.

The current events have nothing to do with a desire to infringe on the interests of Ukraine and the Ukrainian people. They are connected with the defending Russia from those who have taken Ukraine hostage and are trying to use it against our country and our people.

I reiterate: we are acting to defend ourselves from the threats created for us and from worse peril than what is happening now. I am asking you, however hard this may be, to understand this and to work together with us so as to turn this tragic page as soon as possible and to move forward together, without allowing anyone you interfere in our affairs and our relations but developing them independently, so as to create favorable conditions for overcoming all these problems and to strengthen us from within as a single whole, despite the existence of state borders. I believe in this, in our common future.

I would also like to address the military personnel of the Ukrainian Armed Forces.

Comrade officers,

Your fathers, grandfathers and great-grandfathers did not fight the Nazi occupiers and did not defend our common Motherland to allow today`s neo-Nazis to seize power in Ukraine. You swore the oath of allegiance to the Ukrainian people and not to the junta, the people`s adversary which is plundering Ukraine and humiliating the Ukrainian people.

I urge you to refuse to carry out their criminal orders. I urge you to immediately lay down arms and go home. I will explain what this means: the military personnel of the Ukrainian army who do this will be able to freely leave the zone of hostilities and return to their families.

I want to emphasise again that al responsibility for the possible bloodshed will lie fully and wholly with the ruling Ukrainian regime.

I would now like to say something very important for those who may be tempted to interfere in these developments from the outside. No matter who tries to stand in our way or all the more so create threats for our country and our people, they must know that Russia will respond immediately, and the consequences will be such as you have never seen in your entire history. No matter how the events unfold, we are ready. All the necessary decisions in this regard have been taken. I hope that my words will be heard."

The rest of the speech is addressed to Russians. (President of Russia, 2022)

The perspective and the message

This is a speech that goes a long way to explain why the war became an imperative. Putin refers to the many interventions the United States has made in other countries. This is knowledge we have in the West, but it is rarely said so explicitly, except for politicians on the left, most often by politicians without power in any government. The fact that it is not an issue to a greater extent in the US and Europe shows the power the United States has over the narrative of the United States as the good policeman in the world.

President Putin mentions bluntly the many interventions. He can be compared to the boy in the fairy tale by Hans Christian Andersen who says that the emperor does not wear clothes. He is also brutal with words when he describes how allies bow to the Americans' policies, even though they are only about the Americans' interests.

The speech provides a justification for the war.
The current head of the CIA, William Burns,
warned as early as 2008 against including
Ukraine in NATO. This became first known
through Wikileaks and has never been denied by
the US authorities. William Burns was the then
the American ambassador to Russia. In the
memorandum in which Burns wrote "Njet means
njet"(no means no) Burns wrote that the
annexation of Ukraine could lead to civil war
with the result that Russia intervened on behalf
of Eastern Ukraine. This was confirmed in
President Putin's speech on the first day of the
invasion.

The rhetoric of the speech

This speech is very factual. It is without filler
words or beautiful formulations intended for the
audience. President Putin gives a factual speech
without insignificant points. Most often he
speaks within the framework of the logos of
rhetoric.

In Russia, Putin has a great support among the
population. He is a popular president, most likely
for a real majority in Russia, although we do not

have exact figures for the popularity of the Russian president. However, in such a context, Putin by the virtue of his person and his position as the president of Russia, has the ethos of rhetoric. Ethos can be explained as: The speaker establishes a sense of persuasion using their own credibility, status, professionalism, research, or credibility of their sources. For the audience in Western countries, on the other hand, President Putin has a low status. Few want to read the whole speech. The views are therefore influenced by the clips that the media reproduce. In the Norwegian media, the speech was portrayed as hostile and threatening.

If you had listened to the speech without prejudices, you would probably say that it was factual, credible and full of meaning. How we perceive the speech is nevertheless largely about

Fig 5 A model of the speech and perceived ethos in the audience in Russia and the West

how we perceive President Putin. For most Russians, he has the ethos of rhetoric. For people in Western countries, one is either indifferent to Putin or negative, then except for the minority in the West who support him.

A strong and ambiguous threat

At the end of the speech, Putin said:

"I would like to say something very important for those who may be tempted to interfere in these developments from the outside. No matter who tries to stand in our way or all the more so create threats for our country and our people, they must know that Russia will respond immediately, and the consequences will be such as you have never seen in your entire history. No matter how the events unfold, we are ready. All the necessary decisions in this regard have been taken. I hope that my words will be heard,"

This paragraph comes at the end of the part of the speech directed at the military personnel in Ukraine. This is a clear threat from Putin. At the same time, he does not say clearly what the threat entails, except that it would be worse than anyone had previously seen. The media speculated about this threat. It was quickly linked to the danger of the use of nuclear weapons. Here, of course, President Putin, bears a great deal of responsibility for the formulations that triggered the speculation. It was not responsible rhetoric, unlike the most important part of Putin`s speech.

Summary

Putin gave a very thorough speech on the first day of the invasion. In the Western media, it has largely been caricatured, smaller parts have been taken out of the context. It is therefore important to analyze the entire speech. This is in stark contrast to leaders in Europe and the President of EU, Ursula von der Leyen, who spoke about the war being about Ukraine`s democracy. And a battle between free democracies and unfree, authoritarian countries.

President Putin justifies the invasion both with the lawlessness the US has shown in other countries and the establishment of US/NATO on the border of Russia, partly with help of neo-Nazis.

Putin gives a speech where the logos of rhetoric are most important. He can reach a Russian audience through his popularity and credibility.

For a Western audience, he has little appeal. There is only a minority in the West who support President Putin. Therefore, he cannot count on a sympathetic audience. At the same time,the

Western audience is largely dependent on how the media conveys Putin`s speeches.

In the West, many were frightened by the speech. This is due to both Putin`s threat, and the media's speculation about what it could be. Putin did not say it specifically, and thus bears a great deal of the responsibility for the media`s speculation about the possible use of nuclear weapons.

The interview with Tucker Carlson?

Introduction

When Oriana Fallaci (1929-2006) interviewed controversial heads of state, she became an even bigger celebrity as a journalist. When Tucker Carlson managed to get an interview with President Putin after three years, there was little recognition in the international community. However, the interview was quickly seen by several millions.

It was a real feat of Tucker Carlson to get to interview President Putin. He worked hard to make it happen, even when he was a news anchor at Fox News.

It was an unusual interview. It showed a president who did not let himself be directed by a journalist, even though Tucker Carlson is one of the most famous journalists on earth today.

The interview

I will reproduce parts of the interview and comment between the various parts of the interview.

Tucker Carlson: "Mr. President, thank you.

On February 24, 2022, you addressed your country in your nationwide address when the conflict in Ukraine started and you said that you were acting because you had come to the conclusion that the United States through NATO might initiate a quote, "surprise attack on our country". And to American ears that sound paranoid. Tell us why you believe the United States might strike Russia out of the blue. How did you conclude that?"

President Putin: "It`s not that the United States was going to launch a surprise strike on Russia. I didn`t say so. Are we having a talk show or a serious conversation?"

Tucker Carlson. «That was a good quote. Thank you. It`s formidably serious!"

Here, President Putin begins to take control of the interview. Given the circumstances, it is not particularly surprising that Tucker Carlson let Putin talk about the origins of Ukraine and Russia, mostly about the story of Ukraine. I know the history of Ukraine. For the audience that probably most of all wanted to hear Putin, the long story about Ukraine was probably unexpected. And perhaps difficult to follow. At the same time, Putin is a convincing and confident narrator. Admittedly, several media reported that Putin was boring and that he did not know history. And similar descriptions. And even for the gifted journalist, Tucker Carlson, it was hard to keep up. Carlson asked:

"I beg your pardon, can you tell us what period….I am losing track where in history we are."

Vladimir Putin: "It was in the 13th century."

Putin`s lecture on history explains some of the background for the current conflict in and about Ukraine. He also says that the German politician

Egon Bahr (SPD) understood Russia`s security needs after the dissolution of the Soviet Union. According to Putin, Egon Bahr said: "If NATO expands, everything would be just the same as during the Cold War, only closer to Russia`s borders."

President Putin says in a reply to Carlson that he believes the West fears China to a far greater extent than Russia. He thus dismisses Tucker Carlson`s claim that it is the other way around.

Putin continues:

"Let`s not talk about who is afraid of whom, let`s not reason in such terms. And let`s get into the fact that after 1991, when Russia expected that it would be welcomed into the brotherly family of "civilized nations" nothing like that happened. You tricked us (I don`t mean you personally when I say you "of course". I`m talking about the United States), the promise was that NATO would not expand eastward, but it happened five times, there were five waves of expansion. We tolerated all that, we were trying to persuade them, we were saying: "Please don`t, we are as bourgeois now as you are, we are a market economy, and there is no Communist party power. Let`s negotiate."

Moreover, I have also said this publicly before (let`s look at Yeltsin`s times now), there was a moment when a certain rift started growing between us. Before that, Yeltsin came to the United States, remember, he spoke in the Congress and said the good words: "God bless America." Everything he said were signals-let us in."

Putin then describes the conflict that arose when Yeltsin championed the cause of the Serbs during the war in the former Yugoslavia. What did the Americans do then, Putin asked rhetorically? "In violation of international law and the UN Charter it started bombing Belgrade".

Later in the interview Putin says:

"Well. I became President in 2000. I thought okay, the Yugoslav issue is over, but we should try to restore relations. Let`s reopen the door that Russia had to go through. And moreover I`ve said it publicly. I can reiterate. At a meeting here in the Kremlin with the outgoing President Bill Clinton, right here in the next room, I said to him, I asked him. "Bill, do you think if Russia asked to join NATO, do you think it would happen? Suddenly he said:" You know, it's interesting, I think yes". But in the evening, when we had dinner, he said: "You know, I`ve talked to my team, no-no, it's not possible now".

The entire interview is available on the website of "The President of Russia". The interview shows a Russia that wanted cooperation from the US but was not met with sufficient respect.

What can we learn from the interview?

First and foremost, the interview is different from similar interviews in Western countries. In Western media, journalists often place themselves in a more important role than the person they interview. President Putin showed that he wanted to be an equal and take part in the conducting of the interview. At the same time, he politely answered all questions he had an answer to. Tucker Carlson as a journalist had limited leeway since he was, in a sense, a guest of the President of Russia. In Kremlin. In the very heart of power in Russia.

The interview should provide diplomats and negotiators with a solid basis for negotiations about peace. The global we – if there is such a thing – does not have to agree with what President Putin says, but it is a very good beginning for further discussions about Russia`s place in the world, Ukraine, peace, international cooperation and international security.

Although Putin throughout his time as president has built an image as the strong man, the strong head of state, he shows once again that he and Russia have been rejected by the West. There is no doubt that President Putin wanted closer cooperation with the West, but for various reasons, perhaps most of all the Americans politics on power, Russia was never invited into the warmth of the West.

Summary

This is a very interesting interview, Although Putin revealed few news. Nevertheless, what Putin said was interesting for the understanding of Russia, Putin, the conflict over Ukraine and the relationship with the West.

Perhaps, the most important thing about the interview is that the person who was interviewed- President Putin- wanted to have influence over the interview. Nevertheless, there were both very interesting questions and answers throughout the interview.

Speech after the terror attack in the Crocus City Hall

Introduction

The attack on Crocus City Hall was dramatic. At least 144 people were killed. Hundreds were injured in March 2024.The alleged perpetrators were caught while they were fleeing Russia. There was quickly much speculations about who had facilitated the attack with money and weapons. For Russia as a nation, it was a terrible attack on the country`s population. Here is the speech President Putin gave after the terror attack:

The speech

"I am addressing you today in connection with a horrific and savage act of terrorism, which claimed the lives of dozens of peaceful, innocent people- our compatriots, including children, teenagers, and women. Doctors are fighting to save the lives of the victims in critical conditions. I am confident that they will do everything within their power, and even beyond, to preserve the lives and health of all those injured. I extend my heartfelt gratitude to ambulance crews, air ambulance teams, special forces, fire fighters, and rescuers, who made every effort to save lives and rescue people from the gunfire, from the epicentre of fire and smoke, preventing even greater losses.

I cannot but acknowledge the help provided by ordinary citizens who, in the immediate aftermath of the tragedy, did not remain indifferent or apathetic and provided first aid and transported the victims to the hospitals, working alongside doctors and special agencies personnel.

We will provide the necessary support to all families whose lives have been affected by this horrible atrocity, to the wounded and the injured. I express my deepest and most sincere condolences to all those who have lost their loved ones. The entire country, all our people are grieving together with you. I declare March 24 a day of national mourning.

Additional anti-terrorist and anti-sabotage measures have been introduced in Moscow, the Moscow Region, and all regions of the country. Our top priority now is to prevent those behind the blood massacre from committing another crime.

Regarding the investigation of the crime and the results of the operational search action, we can currently say the following. All four perpetrators, who were directly involved in the terrorist attack, all those who shot and killed people, have been found and apprehended. They attempted to escape and were heading towards Ukraine, where, according to preliminary information, a window was prepared for them on the Ukrainian side to cross the state border. A total of 11 people have been detained. The Federeal Security Service and other Law enforcement agencies are working diligently to identify and expose the accomplice base behind these terrorists: those who provided them with transport, planned escape routes from the crime scene, and prepared caches with weapons and ammunition.

The investigative and law enforcement agencies will spare no effort to establish all the details of this crime. However, it is already clear that we are confronted not simply with a carefully and cynically planned terrorist attack, but a premeditated and organized mass murder of peaceful, defenceless people. The perpetrators cold-bloodedly and deliberately targeted our citizens, including our children, with the intent to kill them at close range. Like the Nazis who once carried out massacres in the occupied territories, they planned to stage a demonstrative execution, a bloody act of intimidation.

All perpetrators, organisers and masterminds of this crime will face fair and inevitable punishment, whoever they may be and whoever directed them. I emphasise one more. We will identify and bring to justice each and every individual who stands behind these terrorists, those who orchestrated the atrocity, the assault against Russia and our people.

We understand what the terrorist threat means. In this regard, we rely on cooperation with all states that sincerely share our pain and are ready to really join forces in the fight against a common enemy, international terrorism and all its manifestations.

Terrorists, murderers, those inhumane individuals who have no nationality and cannot have one, face one and the same gloomy prospect - retribution and oblivion. They have no future. Our common duty now, shared by our comrades - in-arms at the front and all citizens of our country, is to stand united as one. I am confident that we will, for nothing and no one can shake our unity and will, our determination and courage, the strength of the united people of Russia. No force will be able to sow the poisonous seeds of discord, panic or disunity in our multi-ethnic society.

Russia has weathered the most arduous, sometimes unbearable trials more than once, yet it has emerged even stronger. And so it shall be now, as well."

What does Putin emphasize in his speech?

Putin draw a line where he says the "horrific and savage attack" and indeed it was. Putin's speech is very different from the speeches that former Prime Minister Jens Stoltenberg gave after the terrorist attack that was committed by a Norwegian against his own people in 2011. At that time, Jens Stoltenberg emphasized soft values. President Putin, on the other hand, prefer to show that the state of Russia can respond with professionalism in the investigation of the terrorist attack.

The population becomes afraid when there has been a terrorist attack. While heads of state in Europe are afraid to offend population groups that may stand behind the attacks, they choose a soft approach. President Putin on the other hand, shows that he is the confident leader who will ensure security in his country. And an investigation of everyone who was behind the terrorist attack.

Putin used few words to show concern for the victims. He only said the most important words to show that he understood. The most important message in the speech was that they should ensure investigations and punishment and that the population could trust that Russia through its leader is in safe hands.

Summary

In his speech he shows different sides of his leadership and rhetoric. He shows concern for the victims and those affected. He shows concern and care for the victims with few words. Indirectly, however, he shows concern for the people by telling what the state of Russia will do after the terrorist attack.

Putin on escalation

Introduction

President Putin commented on the West`s many plans about the war at a press conference on a state visit to Uzbekistan on May 28, 2024. This is a different format than the big speeches. This is important as well as relevant after 27 months of war, and since it again is a danger of a dangerous confrontation between Russia and the United States.

Putin words about escalation

"With regard to the strikes, frankly, I am not sure what the NATO Secretary General is talking about. When he was Prime Minister of Norway, we communicated and addressed challenging issues concerning the Barents Sea and other issues, and generally, we were able to come to terms, and I am positive he was not suffering from dementia back then. If he is talking about potentially attacking Russia's territory with long-range precision weapons, he, as a person who heads a military-political organization, even though he is a civilian like me, should be aware of the fact that long-range precision weapons cannot be used without space-based reconnaissance. This is my first point.

My second point is that the final target selection and what is known as launch mission can only be made by highly skilled specialist who rely on this reconnaissance data, technical reconnaissance data. For some attack systems, such as Storm Shadow, these launch missions can be put in automatically, without the need to use Ukrainian military. Who does it? Those who manufacture and those who allegedly supply these attack systems to Ukraine do. This can and does not happen without the participation of the Ukrainian military. Launching other systems, such as ATACMS, for example, also relies on space reconnaissance data, targets are identified and automatically communicated to the relevant crews that may not even realize what exactly they are putting in. A crew, maybe even a Ukrainian crew, then puts in the corresponding launch mission. However, the mission is put together by representatives of NATO countries, not the Ukrainian military.

So, these officials from NATO countries, especially the based in Europe, particularly in small European countries, should be fully aware of what is at stake. They should keep in mind that theirs are small and densely populated countries, which is a factor to reckon with before they start talking about striking deep into the Russian territory. It is a serious matter and, without a doubt, we are watching very carefully" (President of Russia, 30 May, 2024).

A clear message. Calm and angry

President Putin masters the format of the press conference very well. He is calm and relaxed, but also irritated by NATO and new measures for warfare in Russia. He speaks matter-of-factly about the use of weapons against Russia. He goes outside the unofficial protocol when he indirectly says that the Secretary of NATO has dementia. He also hints at how easy it is to attack small, densely populated countries but without directly saying that Russia will do so.

Questions from President Putin to the West

During the question-and answer session, Putin posed questions to the West. These are both questions and rhetorical questions.

"Look at what your Western colleagues are reporting. No one is talking about shelling Belgorod or other adjacent territories. The only thing they are talking about is Russia opening a new front and attacking Kharkov. Not a word. Why is that? They did with their own hands. Well, let them reap the fruits of their ingenuity. The same thing can happen in case long- range precision weapons which you asked about is used.

More broadly, this unending escalation can lead to serious consequences. If Europe were to face those serious consequences, what will the United States do, considering our strategic arms parity? It is hard to tell.

Are looking for a global conflict? I think they wanted to agree upon strategic arms, but we do not really see them being really eager to do so. They are talking about it but are not doing much to make it happen. We will wait and see what happens next".

Important questions about a possible further escalation

Putin blames the West for the one-sided reporting from the war. He also questions what the West really wants, and whether they see the consequences of what they are doing. The questions Putin is asking should really have been asked by Western leaders too. But one largely avoids discussing the consequences of an escalation of the war. This is therefore a ball that the West should welcome. What is really the strategy behind the constant escalation of the war? These are important questions that the West neglects to ask. Western leaders have locked themselves into a perspective where Putin and Russia are entirely to blame for the war.

Summary

This short chapter deals with the questions with the most explosive power, especially in 2024. The US and NATO have had several agendas with the conflict over Ukraine, which caused Russia to invade Ukraine. Russia has prepared for the possibility of a major war, but President Putin does not want that. The questions about the escalation point to that. In the West, the debate about the escalation of the war seems to have neither a beginning nor an end. There is not a climate for questioning and debating what the strategy is with an escalation of the war by sending long- range missiles into Russia, and what that means in the continuation of the war.

Us and President Putin

Introduction

The title of this book is "President Vladimir Putin and us". In this chapter, I turn the perspective from Putin to us. President Putin is struggling to reach the population in the West. His words must pass through layers of propaganda and what in the field of communication is referred to as noise. What, then, is my purpose for this chapter? What do I want to tell? What would I encourage readers to see?

Hegemonic thinking in the West

The United States has dominated the world after the Second World War. The former Soviet Union did not receive sufficient recognition for their important contribution to Allied victory in 1945. In Europe and the United States, the US and

Great Britain were the victors. This has characterized Western thinking right up to the present day. The Soviet Union`s efforts and great sacrifices during the Second World War have not been communicated in a fair way in the West. This, of course, must be seen in the context of the Soviet Union`s oppression of States in Eastern Europe after the Second World War. They were forced into a communist system of rule. This probably contributed to the Soviet Union quickly going from ally to enemy. After the fall of the Wall in Berlin, both the Soviet Union and the Warsaw Pact were dissolved.

The fall of the Berlin Wall and the dissolution of the Soviet Union contributed to peace and optimism for the future in Europe. The former Soviet Union as the oppressor of the countries of Eastern Europe was largely over, although the liberation of the Baltic states did not happen without a struggle. Russia had not completely freed itself from the mentality of the Soviet Union, even though the union had ceased.

President Yeltsin

President Yeltsin (1931-2007) was popular in the West. He mismanaged the country he led and was anything but a good leader for Russia. He also gave far too much freedom to Russian oligarchs and Western financial advisers, who actually exploited Russia more than they contributed positively to Russia`s transition to capitalism. In the West, it was popular that President Yeltsin did not make demands on the investors, which contributed to toppling the Russian economy.

When President Yeltsin was on state visit to Norway in 1996, he took Queen Sonja and Prime Minister Gro Harlem Brundtland under his arms. He licked around his mouth and said "raspberries with cream" in Russian. The incident went around the world. In Norway, people laughed of the episode. This says something about the low expectations one had of President Yeltsin.

When Putin took over as leader of Russia in 2000, he was met with positive, but not high expectation. Putin was positive to cooperation with both Europe and the United States. He even asked if Russia could join NATO. Then he got no as an answer. Putin wanted close cooperation with the West, He only got it to a certain extent. When Americans were hit by terror on September 11,2001, President Putin offered help to the United States. Putin had served in the former East Germany and was no stranger to other countries. In his first years as president, he reached out both to the United States and Europe.

The war in Iraq – the beginning of a new hostility between Russia and the US

Russia, France and Russia were opposed to the invasion of Iraq. Iraq was also an important ally for Russia in the Middle East. Russia, France and Germany all warned the US against invading Iraq. The US did not listen to the objections and invaded Iraq in 2003. Several have said that this created a lasting divide and destroyed the dialogue between the US and Russia.

The war hawks (neocons)

While European countries breathed a sigh of relief after the fall of the Berlin Wall, and reduced their defense budgets, the American war hawks took a very different approach. The war hawks in Washington, who wield considerable influence in both the Democratic Party and the Republican Party, saw the dissolution of the Soviet Union and the fall of the Wall in Berlin as a victory – for the United States and the West.

The war hawks in Washington did not see that the dissolution of the Soviet Union was a deliberate policy. The war hawks in Washington saw Russia as weak, which in their perspective provided opportunities for the United States.

The war hawks in the United States consist of a group of politicians and employees in the government apparatus. They are often referred to as neocons. It is partly a misleading term. This group had root in conservative politics but stands for radical and imperialistic politics today. The neoconservatives have been the war hawks in Washington for the past 30 years. After Nine Eleven, the terrorist attack was used as a pretext for the wars in Iraq and Afghanistan.

Russia was extremely weak after the dissolution of the Soviet Union. The transition from state economy to capitalism was a disaster. Russia was exposed to an unprecedented predatory economy. They received a lot of bad advice in the 1990s. A few Russians and Westerners enriched themselves beyond decency on Russia`s transition from a planned economy to capitalism.

Russia was no threat to Europe after the dissolution of the Soviet Union. Nevertheless, the expansion of NATO began, as if Russia was a threat to Europe. American leaders had promised not to expand NATO eastwards after Germany was reunited. They broke the promise time and time again and included more and more countries from the former Warsaw Pact into NATO.

Europe in denial?

Europe is in many ways the most enlightened continent in the world. The cradle of knowledge in many fields lies in Europe. At the same time, Europe can be so complete superficial when it comes to important issues such as the war in Ukraine. On May 31, I posted a video with President Putin on twitter X from the press conference in Uzbekistan on May 28, 2024. There. Putin answers important questions about the escalation with long-rage missiles inside

Russia, and what it entails. It should interest all Europeans what Putin said. What people were thinking, I can`t know. There were no likes or comments. In addition, several people unfollowed me on twitter X. On the same day, Ivar Dale in the Norwegian branch of the Helsinki Committee put forward a proposal to cancel the researcher and professor Glenn Diesen. I asked why. After a short time, I was harassed by two men. On of them said I was small and insignificant. The other said I was confused. A third said something even worse. The discourse on the war in Ukraine is rarely – if never wise and enlightened on Norwegian twitter X.

These examples from twitter X are of course not significant. It`s more like the chef sticking his finger into the soup. The chef`s finger in the soup is neither research nor valid. However, as good a chef can know whether the soup is good or not based on a small taste, also a small test can explain parts of important questions, even not significant as in proper research.

Summary

If we could turn back the clock, there would be every chance for peace in Europe. Russia was no threat to Europe. Like the United States, Russia has its sphere of influence and need for a security zone. The US and NATO has not respected that.

The invasion of Ukraine started on February 24, 2022. The reason for it began long before. Although I do not defend the invasion of Ukraine, the answers lie in milestone after milestone since the dissolution of the Soviet Union at the end of 1991.

The propaganda tells us that President Putin wants to be Peter the Great. It is probably rather the United States that wants more power than it already has. Ukraine is paying a high price for that now. Even though it is Russia that invaded Ukraine, the United States is not an innocent party of the conflict. Since the 1990s both the United States and NATO have known that constant expansion of NATO would end in a war sooner rather than later. The question Europe should ask is whether Europe has been sufficiently alert regarding these issues all these years.

Summary

My goal with this book was to provide new perspectives on President Putin. A lot has been written about President Putin. Few have tried to look beyond the one-dimensional image of Putin. This is by no means a defense for President Putin. It is rather an attempt of a more realistic approach to a political leader who is highly controversial in the West.

President Barack Obama impressed with his catchy and elegant rhetoric. President Putin has a far more factual and down-to-earth rhetoric. While President Barack Obama could seduce with elegant formulations, Putin is more a man of facts. Big words are not Putin's style.

This is not a biblical interpretation of the man and the politician Vladimir Putin. On the other hand, it is and interpretation that, at best, can open several perspectives on who Putin really is.

If curtains can shield from the sun, propaganda can obscure the truth. Vladimir Putin is no saint. But he is not the monster he is portrayed as in the West either.

And we? Who are we in the encounter with the stranger? President Putin is in many ways a stranger to us in the West. In a way, we have never really been properly introduced. Yet so many people have an opinion about him. There is no basis for calling President Putin a Hitler, Peter the Great or someone who wants to be Peter the Great.

In his speeches President Putin argues based on facts and Russia`s vital interests. His words are not characterized by hidden agendas. We can learn a lot about Putin by reading his speeches. He is clear, almost boring in what he says. But of course, it is far from boring. He is one of the world's foremost leaders, so his words count. The common thread in his speeches is what he regards as important to Russia.

A prison of arguments

Western countries have locked themselves in a prison of arguments with their criticism of the Russian democracy. It`s not perfect, but shouldn`t stop us from seeing other qualities of the political leader Vladimir Putin. And Russia.

Truth and propaganda

The population of the West has been exposed to massive propaganda about President Putin. Something is planned as propaganda. Much is also groupthink, laziness and copying of the one-dimensional description of who President Vladimir Putin is. His speech in Munich in 2007 should have been an acceptable input on international relations and security policy. Instead, the speech made him a pariah in the West. That was both unfair and unwise. The West, and the US in particular, must endure hearing what the world looks like from Moscow. It is tragic that the West turned its back on the knowledge, insight and suggestions in the speech Putin gave on the Security conference in 2007.

Had the West taken him serious then, the war in Ukraine might have been avoided.

In the West, we have long lived in the illusion that the West is the good one. That the United States is like the talented actors Tom Cruise, Harrison Ford and Meryl Streep – and just good. Hollywood has perhaps been more important to our belief in peace and security. And the United States as everyone`s protector. Unlike the truth about war and peace in the world. Putin`s speech in Munich shattered that illusion, even though participants at a security conference often are more realistic than most people.

In Norwegian schools, children and young people learn about the criticism of sources. When it comes to propaganda about Putin, it is often perceived as easily as if it was an ice cream on a summer`s day. The propaganda is often digested without reflection.

In Munich in 2007, President Putin pierced the myth of the West as the good one. The West has not forgiven him for that. Instead of dialogue, confrontation has been chosen.

This book has the title "President Vladimir Putin and us". This title is more a metaphor than a fact. At the same time, it is based on a wish that we should look at how we, the collective West, view President Putin. What pitfalls have vi overlooked?

And let`s hope for more reason and better communication. In the future.

References

Aristoteles (2006) «Retorikk», Vidarforlaget, Oslo, Norway

Associated Press (2019) "Far-right groups protest Ukrainian President`s peace plan", Los Angeles Times, US, Oct.14

Aurelius, Marcus (2016) "Meditations", Dover Publications, New York, US

Barnes, Julian B., Goldman, Adam, Entous, Adam and Schwirtz, Michael (2022) "U.S. Believes Ukrainians Were behind an Assassination in Russia", New York Times, USA, Oct. 5

Berman, Russell (2014) "Poroschenko: Ukraine`s Battle with Russia Is America`s War Too", The Atlantic, Sept.18

Bernsen, Martin "Make Ukraine Great Again (2022)", Weekendavisen, Copenhagen, Denmark, April 2

Bohdanova, Teyana (2014) "Unexpected Revolution: The Role of Social Media in Ukraine`s Euromaidan uprising", Sage Journals

Borup, Birgitte (2022) "Zelenskyj har andre fjender end Putin.Én av dem har nettop vist sit ansigte," Berlingske Tidende, Denmark. March 29

Berbner, Thomas (2015) "Aggressor Putin: die Fehler des Westens", Das Erste, Tyskland

Berman, Russel (2014) "Poroschenko: Ukraine`s Battle with Russia Is "America`s War Too", The Atlantic, Sept. 18

Cohen, Josh (2018)" Ukraine`s neo-Nazi problem", Reuters March 19

Collinson. Stephen (2022) "Zelensky taps national psyches of other countries as he appeals to save his own", CNN Politics March 16

Clausewitz, Carl (1943) "On War", Wordsworth Editions LTD, UK

Dibb, Paul (2022) "Why did Russia attack Ukraine and what are its geopolitical implications?", ANU Public lecture, Australia

Freeman, Ben (2022) "Ukrainian lobbyists mounted unprecedented campaign on U.S. lawmakers in 2021", The Intercept, US

Fridman, Lex (2022) Vladimir Putin and War in Ukraine, interview with Oliver Stone, lexfridman.com

Fried, Daniel and Volker, Kurt (2022) "The Speech in Which Putin Told us Who He Was", Politico, February 18

Gallo, Carmine (2022) "Zelensky`s Audience-Centered Speeches Connect to Shared Values", Forbes, Jersey City, USA, March 17

Gardner, Stephen (2023) "Douglas Mcgregor: Ukraine will be destroyed", Youtube, March 1

Gov.uk (2022)"PM call with President Macron: 6 May 2022", Press release from the British Government

Garsten, Bryan (2009)" Saving Persuasion» «A defense of Rhetoric and Judgement", Harvard University Press

Gessen, Masha (2022)" Putin Mannen uten ansikt», RIVERHEAD BOOKS, The Penguin Group

Haas, Richard and Kupchan, Charles (2023)" Redefining Success in Ukraine" "A New Strategy Must balance Means and Ends" Foreign Affairs, November 17

Herb, Jeremy (2022) "Exclusive: Zelensky says world should be prepared for the possibility Putin use nuclear weapons", CNN April 15

Hersh, Seymour (2023) "How America Took Out The Nord Stream Pipeline", Substack

ISW (2022-2023)

Janis, Irving Lester (1982) "Groupthink", Houghton Miffin

Johanneson, Kurt (2005) "Svensk retorik" "Från medeltiden til våra dager", Norstedts, Sweden

Kessler, Glenn (2022) «Zelensky`s famous quote of "need ammo, not a ride, not easily confirmed", The Washington Post, USA, March 6

Kirby, Paul (2023) "Ukraine billionaire Ihor Kolomoisky targeted in new anti-corruption swoop", BBC News, Febr. 1

Koppang, Haavard (2009) "Social Influence by Manipulation: A Definition and Case of Propaganda", Middle East Critique

Klemperer, Victor (2010) «LTI» «Notisbuch eines Philologen», Reclam, Stuttgart, Germany

Lai, Linda (1999) "Dømmekraft" Tano Aschehoug, Oslo, Norway

Lazar, Nomi Claire (2022) "Need an expert? War in Ukraine: President. Volodymyr Zelensky`s rhetoric", University of Ottawa, Canada

Lopatonok, Igor (2019) "Revealing Ukraine", Producer Oliver Stone

Machiavelli, Niccolò (1513,1993) "The Prince", SD Books

Malan, Lucio (2011) "Post – orange Ukraine: Internal dynamics and foreign priorities", Report to the NATO Parliamentary Assembly

McEnerney, Larry (2023)" The Gettysburg Address", European Speechwriter Network

Melkozerova, Veronika (2023)" Defense minister Reznikov under fire as corruption probes rock Ukraine", politico.eu January 23rd

McGovern, Ray (2023) "Is Biden being Misinformed on Ukraine & China", Judging Freedom, April 17

Mcgregor, Douglas (2023) "Everything is Pure Ukraine Propaganda !!! Russians Fire 60,000 Artillery Rounds", Finance Mail

Mcgregor, Douglas (2023) "Ukraine is About to be ANNIHILATED", Stephen Gardner podcast.

Mcgregor, Douglas (2023) "The Gathering Storm", The American Conservative, USA, March 14

Napolitano, Andrew (2023) "Ukraine- What Offensive can we Expect? Tony Shaffer", Judging Freedom, USA

Napolitano, Andrew (2023) "Ukraine War, What´s Next?" with Phil Giraldi, Judging Freedom, April 25

Mc Govern, Ray (2023) «The Banality of Biden`s Advisers", Judging Freedom, March 28

Minakov, Mykhailo (2021) "Just like All the Others: The End of the Zelensky Alternative?" Focus Ukraine, Wilson Center, Nov. 2

Müller, Jan-Werner (2017) "Hvad er populisme?", Informations Forlag, Copenhagen, Denmark

Obama, Barack (2022)" Disinformation & democracy", Stanford University, California

Pifer, Steven (2020) "Ukraine`s Zelensky ran on a reform platform-Is he delivering, The Brooking Institution, July 22

Pollen, Geir (2021) "Volga" "En russisk reise", Gyldendal, Norway

Pozner, Vladimir (2018) "How the United States Created Vladimir Putin", Yale University, US, September 27

President of Russia, http://en.kremlin.ru

Putin, Vladimir (2007) "Speech and the Following Discussion at the Munich Conference on Security Policy", http://en.kremlin.ru February 10

Putin, Vladimir (2023) "Annual speech to Russian general assembly", The Telegraph, February 21

Sakwa, Richard (2021) «Frontline Ukraine» «Crisis in the borderlands", Bloomsbury Academic

Sayers, Freddie (2023) «Who really blew up the Nordstream 2 pipeline?", interview with Jeffrey Sachs, Feb.15

Von der Schulenburg, Michael, Funke. Hajo, Kujat, Harald (2023) „Frieden für Ukraine", Brave New Europe, UK, November 4

Smith-Meyer, Bjarke (2023) „NATO should be ready for "bad news" from Ukraine, Stoltenberg warns", Politico, December 3

Skagen. Kaj (2023) «Raudt mot røkla», Dag og Tid, Feb.3

Steinfeld, Hans Wilhelm (2009) «Hatet i Europa» «Tyve år etter Berlins andre fall», Cappelen Damm, Oslo, Norway

Stoltenberg, Jens (2022,2023) „Speeches", NATO https://www.nato.int

Stoltenberg, Jens (2023) Speech upon receiving the American Academy of Berlin`s 2023 Henry A. Kissinger Prize, Nov. 10

Spiegel Gespräch (2023) " Olaf, hör zu, uns fehlen Raketen", Der Spiegel, Germany Nov.7

Strøm, Ole Kristian (2023) „Prigozjin: -Vi er lovet nok ammunisjon», VG, Norway. May 7

Thakur, Ramesh (2023) «What are the possible endgames in the Ukraine war?", The Japan Times, Japan Feb. 3

Thomassen, Åse (2017) «Politikk retorikk populisme», Protence Forlag, Oslo, Norway

Thomassen, Åse (2022) «War and rhetoric", Kindle Amazon, US

Thomassen Åse (2023) "Krigsspillet Russland - Ukraina", Protence Forlag, Oslo, Norway

Thorndike, Edward Lee (1970) "Educational Psychology The psychology of learning", Volume 2, Greenwood Press, US

Transparency International (2021) "Corruption Perceptions Index"

Transparency International Ukraine

Trump Donald (2018) "Stoltenberg er min største fan", VG TV July 6. Oslo Norway

Tunander, Ola (2023)" Vår vei til atomkrigen, Vardøger nr. 40

"Ukraine crisis: Transcript of leaked Nuland-Pyatt call" (2014) BBC News, February 7

Yerushalmy, Jonathan (2023) "Russia planning major offensive to mark first anniversary of war: Ukraine defence minister", The Guardian, UK, February 2

Von der Buchard, Hans (2023)" Brazil`s Lula snubs Olaf Scholz with Ukraine war remarks". Politico, Jan 31

Webber, Esther (2022) "Boris Johnson warns against seeking "bad peace in Ukraine", Politico, June 23

Wertheim, Stephen (2022)" The One key Word Biden Needs to invoke on Ukraine", The Atlantic, June 11

«Taler som forandret verden" (2009), «Speeches that Changed the World», Forlaget Press, Oslo, Norway

The Economist (2022) «Confidence from the bunker», The Economist April 2

Transparency International (2022) «The State of corruption: Armenia, Azerbaijan, Georgia, Moldova and Ukraine".

"Ukraine conflict: Russian forces attack from three sides", BBC News, Febr. 24, 2022

Weber, Max (1982)" Makt og byråkrati, Gyldendal, Oslo, Norway

Zelensky, Volodymyr (2022) "A message from Ukraine", Hutchinson Heinemann

Zelensky, Volodymyr (2023) "Zelensky addresses Parliament", Washington Post, Feb. 8

Concepts in rhetoric

Actio: Presentation. Use of body language.

Ad hominem: Argument directed at a person rather than the position they are in.I t is used to counter an argument. In the debate over Ukraine, terms such as "Putinist" (in Norway) or "pro-Russia" are often used to degrade those who do not uncritically support Ukraine.

Allegory: A story or image. Figurative speech. Plato`s parable of the cave is a well-known allegory in rhetoric and philosophy.

Alliteration: Words with the same letter or sound. Example: The barbarians broke through the barricade.

Allusion: An allusion is an allusion to commonly known persons or quotes. In Western Culture, there are often references to Greek mythology or the bible. Florence Nightingale and Nelson Mandela are examples of people that many associate with certain qualities and values.

Anaphora: The repetition of words at the beginning of successive clauses, phrases, or sentences. It is often used to emphasize a message or to make their words memorable. It can also have a suggestive effect.

Antithesis: Opposition, or contrast of ideas or words.

Aptus: Message tailored to the audience.

Argumentum ad baculum: Intimidation or creating fear.

Argumentum ad hominem: Unreasonable arguments. Personal attacks. Appealing to feelings or prejudices rather than intellect.

Argumentum ad populum: Popularity argument. Something everybody knows.

Attentus: Make the listener aware.

Benevolus: Kind, friendly, favorable.

Chiasm: A writing style that uses a unique repetition pattern for clarification.

Climax: Arrangements of words, phrases, or clauses in an order of ascending strength.

Contra: Contradict. Opposing.

Copia: Study others to imitate. Speechwriters say many politicians want to sound like former President Barack Obama. Others have other role models.

Docili: Make the audience aware of the topic.

Dubiato: When the speaker pretends, he or she is uncertain or doubtful.

Elocutio: The skill of a clear and expressive speech: Pronunciation and articulation are of great importance.

Ethos: The speaker establishes a sense of persuasion using their own credibility, status, professionalism, research, or credibility of their sources.

Euphism: Substitution of an agreeable or at least non-offensive expression for one whose plainer meaning might be harsh or unpleasant.

Exordium: Introduction. Beginning.

Fallacies: Errors in reasoning that will undermine the logic of your argument. Example: It is snowing. That is a proof that there is no global warming. Look! Or: President Zelensky is a Jew. There is no fascism in Ukraine.

Halo effect: A first impression that embellishes the later experiences with the same person. President Zelensky made a strong impression on people in Western countries after February 24, 2022. The fact that he was later able to do many mistakes without being criticized can be an example of halo effect.

Hyperbole: A deliberate and obvious exaggeration. Example: He made the moon.

Intellectio: The situation is analyzed. Where do we stand with the target group, who are we addressing? This is where we formulate our message.

Interogatio: A rhetorical question.

Inventio: The first of five cannons of rhetoric: the discovery of the resources for persuasion. Cicero defined invention as the discovery of valid or seemingly valid arguments to render one`s cause probable.

Inversion: Replacing words into sentences. Example: Good communication is the result of credibility. Credibility is the result of good communication.

Kairos: It`s about finding the right words at the right time or situation. Example: President Zelensky said he needed ammo not a ride.

Litotes: It is a rhetorical figure in which one expresses the opposite of what most of us see and mean. Litotes is a form of understatement. Putin is not a little cat.

Logos: Logos is about reason and objectivity. The logical argument.

Metaphor: A metaphor is a figure of speech for a rhetorical effect. An implied comparison achieved through a figurative use of words. The words are not used in it`s literal sense, but in one analogous to it. Example: Peace in Ukraine is Peace in Europe.

Oxymoron: Paradox achieved by the juxtaposition of words which seem to contradict one another. Example: War is peace.

Paraphrase: To repeat the same. Say the same thing with new formulations.

Pathos: The speaker communicates through emotions. They talk with the audience in mind. Pathos is using feelings to both appeal and persuade.

Paraphrase: To repeat. Say the same thing with new formulations.

Paradox: An assertation seemingly opposed to common sense, often with some truth in it. Examples. «What a pity that youth must be wasted on the young" (Georg Bernhard Shaw).

Pistis: It`s a kind of persuasion classified by Aristotle: The truth is not provided by the speaker. The proof is known before the speech.

Personification: Give personality to an impersonal thing.

Pleonasm: Use of superfluous words, often enriching thought.

Refutio: Counterargument. Example: You talk like the devil reading the bible.

Rhetorical question: Ask a question assuming the audience knows the answer.

Simile: An explicit comparison between two things using "like" or "as".

Synechdoche: A figure of speech in which a part is made to represent the whole. Example: Her tears said more than words about the situation facing them.

Tricolon: A tricolon is three successive words. Example: Vedi vidi vince. Or God green greed.

Vituperatio: A term describing any speech of blame. Example: President Volodymyr Zelensky blaming President Biden and President Xi for not attending the peace summit in Switzerland in June 2024.